more THAN mud Pies

Group

Loveland, Colorado

MORE THAN MUD PIES

Copyright © 1998 Group Publishing, Inc.

Credits
Contributing Authors: Robin Christy, Kathy Duggan, Nancy Wendland Feehrer,
    Nanette Goings, Barbie Murphy, Dan Nehrbass, and Liz Shockey
Book Acquisitions Editor: Susan L. Lingo
Editor: Beth Rowland Wolf
Quality Control Editor: Paul Woods
Chief Creative Officer: Joani Schultz
Copy Editor: Debbie Gowensmith
Designer and Art Director: Jean Bruns
Cover Art Director: Jeff A. Storm
Cover Designer: Becky Hawley
Computer Graphic Artist: Randy Kady
Cover Illustrator: Shelton Leong
Illustrator: Dana Ragan
Production Manager: Peggy Naylor

Library of Congress Cataloging-in-Publication Data
More than mud pies
        p.   cm.
    ISBN 0-7644-2044-5 (alk. paper)
    1. Christian education of preschool children. 2. Bible crafts.
I. Group Publishing.
BV1475.7.M67 1997
268'.432--dc21
                                                                97-37795
                                                                CIP

10 9 8 7 6 5 4 3 2 1   07 06 05 04 03 02 01 00 99 98
Printed in the United States of America.

Contents

SECTION FOUR: NUMBER SKILLS

Introduction

Preschool children love arts and crafts. They love working with paper and glue and paint to create one-of-a-kind projects that express their creativity. Unfortunately the craft projects preschool children do in church are almost always the two-dimensional, refrigerator-art variety. Too often, these projects never even make it to the refrigerator. Many crafts get tossed in the trash can as soon as families get home from church. A Sunday school teacher might wonder whether the time and expense of art projects are really worthwhile and whether the children are really learning anything.

But in *More Than Mud Pies,* preschool craft projects take on new meaning. In this book you'll find nearly fifty crafts that directly relate to the Scripture lessons and concepts you want children to learn. You'll find crafts about Creation, Noah, God's love for us, and many other key Christian topics. And most of the craft projects are easily adapted to a number of different Bible stories.

You'll find the preschool children in your classroom taking pride in their ability to create fun, cute projects they'll use again and again. That's because the crafts in this book are used to play learning games designed to teach the developmental concepts that preschoolers are learning. With these craft projects, preschoolers will learn colors, counting, language skills, body skills, and thinking skills through easy-to-play games.

With each craft idea, you'll find instructions for a developmental learning game that teaches important concepts and will keep preschoolers engaged, interested, and having fun.

You'll also find a photocopiable set of game instructions that you can send home to parents. The craft projects from your class will no longer be stuck on the refrigerator, set on a shelf—or worse—tossed in the garbage. Parents will be able to teach these skills and concepts to their children at home with the game instructions and the craft project that children have made in class. On the photocopiable game instructions, you can jot down just how the craft project related to the story you taught in class. Thus the learning is reinforced, and parents and children are involved in meaningful activity together.

Use the crafts and games from *More Than Mud Pies* whenever you want to multiply the learning of preschoolers in your classroom.

SECTION ONE:

Language Skills

CRAFT SUMMARY:
Make treasure envelopes to store shapes.

LEARNING GOAL:
To recognize shapes and letters

LESSON CONNECTION:
Use this idea when children are learning about God's love for people.

SPRINKLING OF SUPPLIES:
You'll need poster board, brightly colored construction paper, scissors, tacky craft glue, markers, a paper plate, and craft sticks or cotton swabs. You'll also need a large manila envelope for each child.

PRIOR PREP:
Cut out small circles, squares, rectangles, triangles, and stars from poster board. Write the letters of each child's name on poster board shapes, using one shape per letter and as many different shapes as possible.
For each child, also make an identical set of lettered shapes out of brightly colored construction paper. You should have a set of poster board shapes and a set of construction paper shapes that spell each child's name. Hide all the poster board shapes.
Photocopy the Direction Box from the next page for each child.

Treasure Envelopes

CREATING THE CRAFT

Craft Time: 10 min.

Set out markers and large manila envelopes. Also mix up the construction paper shapes and set them out. Put a small puddle of craft glue on a paper plate, and provide craft sticks or cotton swabs for children to use to apply glue to the construction paper shapes.

Help each child select the letters that spell his or her name. Then encourage children to decorate the outsides of their envelopes with the markers. Help the children glue the construction paper shapes on the outside of their envelopes in the correct order to spell their names.

As the children are decorating their treasure envelopes, ask them to identify the shapes and letters.

Say: **Sometimes we put important things—treasures—in envelopes or boxes to protect them. Each one of you is a treasure to God. You are so important that God sent his own Son to earth for you. Listen to what the Bible says.** Read John 3:16 from an easy-to-understand version of the Bible; then say: **Let's play a game about treasures.**

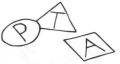

PLAYING THE GAME

Game Time: 15 min.

Have the children hunt for the hidden "treasures"—the poster board letters that match the shapes and letters on the outside of their envelopes.

Explain to children that they should only take one of each lettered shape that they need for their names. Help younger preschoolers find their treasures. After children have found all of the shapes, have them place the poster board lettered shapes on top of the treasure envelope lettered shapes like puzzle pieces. Then have the children put the poster board shapes inside their treasure envelopes for safekeeping.

Be sure to send the treasure envelopes and shapes home along with copies of the Direction Box.

Extension Ideas

● Encourage children to go on a treasure hunt for household items that match the shapes.

● Adapt this activity to use when you're talking about the pearl of great value (Matthew 13:46) or when you're talking about heaven.

Treasure Envelopes

OBJECT: To recognize shapes and letters

1. Hide the lettered poster board shapes.

2. Let your child find all the shapes, identify the shapes and letters, and spell his or her name with the shapes.

3. Try the game in every room in the house!

CRAFT SUMMARY:
Make feathery friends that "fly" up, under, and around.

LEARNING GOAL:
To understand concepts of over, under, between, around, and on

LESSON CONNECTION:
Use this idea when children are learning about Elijah and the ravens.

SPRINKLING OF SUPPLIES:
You'll need large craft sticks, craft feathers, markers, a paper plate, cotton swabs, and tacky craft glue. You'll also need yellow and black construction paper, scissors, and a hole punch.

PRIOR PREP:
Using a hole punch, punch out two circles from the black construction paper for each child. Cut the yellow construction paper into small triangles about one-fourth inch wide. Make one triangle for each child.
Photocopy the Direction Box from the next page for each child.

Feathery Friends

CREATING THE CRAFT

Craft Time: 15 min.

Set out markers and feathers. Put a small puddle of glue on a paper plate, and provide cotton swabs for children to use to apply glue to feathers and paper pieces.

Give each child a craft stick. Have the children decorate their birds with beautiful markings and feathers. Hand out two black construction paper dots and a yellow triangle to each child. Show the children how to glue the paper pieces in place to create eyes and beaks for their feathery friends. Be sure to make your own feathery friend.

TEACHER TIP

Some preschoolers may struggle with the fine motor skills needed to pick up small paper pieces from a table. Show children how to slide the paper dots and triangles from the table into the palms of their hands. Then show them how to cup their hands so the paper pieces "stand up" and are easier to pick up.

While the children are working, say: **When God made the animals, he was very careful to give them everything they needed. God gave birds feathers and wings so they could fly high in the sky. Let's play a game about a Bible story in which birds are very important.**

When children have finished making the feathery friends, play the following learning game together.

Game Time:
10 min.

Have children sit on the floor with their birds. Say: **Elijah was a prophet who gave the people important messages from God. Once Elijah had to hide from a king who didn't like the message. While Elijah was hiding, some birds called ravens did something special. Listen to my words about those ravens, and follow my actions.**

Elijah needed help, so God sent the ravens to help him.
The ravens flew over the trees (fly the bird over your head),
Under a cloud (make a fist in the air, and fly the bird under it),
And between the mountains. (Fly the bird between your knees.)
They flew around Elijah. (Fly the bird around your head.)
They landed next to him (set the bird on the floor next to you),
And they gave him bread and meat to eat. (Touch the bird to your mouth.)

After you've gone through the actions, have the children take turns giving directions for the others to follow. Play until each child has directed the feathery friends in a motion.

Be sure to send the feathery friends home along with copies of the Direction Box.

Feathery Friends

OBJECT: To understand concepts of over, under, between, around, and on

1. Tell this story, and have your child follow the directions with his or her feathery friend.

Elijah needed help, so God sent the ravens to help him.
The ravens flew over the trees (fly bird over your head),
Under a cloud (make a fist; fly bird under your fist),
And between the mountains. (Fly bird between your knees.)
They flew around Elijah. (Fly bird around your head.)
They landed next to him (set bird on the floor next to you),
And they gave him bread and meat to eat. (Touch bird to your mouth.)

2. Let your child suggest motion ideas while you hold the feathery friend. Encourage your child to use words such as over, under, up, and down.

Extension Ideas

● Let the feathery friends take a tour of your church or home. Encourage children to creatively introduce new directions for each room, such as "Have your feathery friend hop in bed for a nap" or "Let your feathery friend sit on the rocking chair."

● You can adapt this activity to use during a lesson about Creation or about the sparrows in Matthew 10:29-31.

Tall-and-Small Friends

CREATING THE CRAFT

Craft Time: 15 min.

Have each child get three paper plates and choose one of the plates to be the "head" of his or her creature. Show children how to use a marker to make eyes, a nose, and a mouth on the plate. As children work, remind them that God created them and shaped them into the special people he wanted them to be.

Hand each child two construction paper strips. Demonstrate how to fold a strip accordion-style by folding one-inch sections back and forth. Help the children fold their strips, crease the folds, and then unfold the strips.

Help children assemble their "friends" by taping a folded paper strip to the bottom of the head. Then have children attach another plate to the end of the strip. Have them place another strip at the bottom of that plate and complete the creature by taping the last plate in place.

When children have finished making the tall-and-small friends, play the following learning game together.

PLAYING THE GAME

Game Time: 10 min.

Have children stand in a circle, holding their friends. Show children how to crouch down with their creatures, making them appear very small. Then show children what happens when they stand up: Their creatures grow tall! Let children practice making their creatures grow from small to tall. Then lead children in the following action rhyme:

> *God loves me when I'm very small* (crouch down, holding your creature to the ground),
> *And he will love me when I'm tall!* (Stretch up as tall as you can while holding your creature up.)
> *When I'm little, God loves me.* (Crouch down again.)
> *And when I'm big as I can be* (stretch up with your creature),
> *Then God will still love me!*

Be sure to send the tall-and-small friends home along with copies of the Direction Box.

Extension Ideas

● Use the tall-and-small friends to help children see how much they've grown. Create a giant creature to use to mark children's heights each month.

● Use this activity when you're teaching children about Luke 2:52: "And Jesus grew in wisdom and stature, and in favor with God and men."

Tall-and-Small Friends

OBJECT: To understand concepts of tall and small

1. Have your child stand, holding the tall-and-small friend. Talk about how tall and small (or short) are opposites.

2. Have your child demonstrate "tall" by standing tall with his or her friend.

3. Have your child demonstrate "small" by crouching down with his or her friend.

4. As you say this rhyme, have your child crouch or stand at the appropriate times.

> *God loves me when I'm very small* (crouch),
> *And he will love me when I'm tall!* (Stand.)
> *When I'm little, God loves me.* (Crouch.)
> *And when I'm big as I can be* (stand),
> *Then God will still love me!*

Rainbow Names

CREATING THE CRAFT

Craft Time: 15 min.

Set out index cards, tape, markers, and alphabet stickers or stencils. Help each child spell his or her name by putting one alphabet sticker on each index card. Older preschoolers may want to write the letters themselves using watercolor markers.

When the letter cards are finished, have each child put the cards in the right order to spell his or her name. Explain to children that in our language letters go from left to right. Then explain that letters can also go from top to bottom. Help the children rearrange the letters of their names in a vertical column and tape the letter cards together.

Give each child one strip of each color of crepe paper. Have the children lay the strips horizontally to the right side of their name cards. Help the children tape the strips to their name cards.

Talk with children about God's "rainbow promise": God promised never to flood the earth again. Also talk about how God cared for Noah and how God knows the children in your class by name and will care for them, too.

When children have finished making the rainbow names, play the following learning game together.

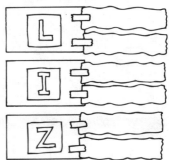

PLAYING THE GAME

Game Time: 10 min.

Have the children sit in a circle and put their rainbow names in front of them. Say: **If your**

name has an "a" in it, stand up and wave your arms. Have children with a's in their names stand up and wave their arms. Then call out another letter and another direction, such as pat your head or wiggle all over. After you've called out several letters from every child's name, invite children to take turns holding up their flags and spelling their names.

Then lead the children in a name parade. Have the children line up and march around the room, waving their flags. Have children "sound off" one at a time, calling out their names and lifting their flags.

Be sure to send the rainbow names home along with copies of the Direction Box.

Extension Idea

● Use this craft in a getting-to-know-you game. Put all the flags letter-side down on the floor, and mix them up. Have a volunteer choose a flag. Identify the name, and then have the child with the flag hand it to the child whose name is on the flag.

Rainbow Names

OBJECT: To recognize letters and names

1. Set the rainbow name in front of you and your child.

2. Say, "If your name has an 'a' in it, stand up and wave your arms."

3. Call out several letters, varying the action each time. If your child has that letter in his or her name, have him or her do the action. If the letter is not in your child's name, have your child shake his or her head "no."

4. When the game ends, have your child spell his or her name aloud while pointing to each letter in the flag.

LEARNING GOAL:
To follow directions and understand the concepts of near and far

LESSON CONNECTION:
Use this idea when children are learning about the sheep following their master (John 10:4).

SPRINKLING OF SUPPLIES:
Empty toilet paper tubes, a hole punch, cotton balls, glue, cotton swabs, scissors, yarn, black construction paper, and newspaper.

PRIOR PREPARATION:
Punch a hole in the end of each toilet paper tube, and tie one end of a six-foot length of yarn through the hole. Cut two ears for each sheep from the black construction paper (see illustration). Cover the art area with newspaper. Photocopy the Direction Box from the next page for each child.

The Shepherd's Sheep

CREATING THE CRAFT

Craft Time:
15 min.

Set out the prepared toilet paper tubes. Show the children how to use the cotton swabs to paint glue on the outside of the tubes. A very thin layer of glue works best. Then help the children cover their tubes with one layer of cotton balls and attach the ears with glue. The ears should go on the same end of the tubes as the string. While the children are working, have them think of names for their sheep. When the sheep are covered with cotton and the ears have been attached, set the sheep aside to dry.

After the shepherd's sheep have dried, play the following learning game together.

PLAYING THE GAME

Game Time:
10 min.

Tell the story of the sheep and their shepherd from John 10. Then have the children stand in a line, shoulder to shoulder, with their sheep on the floor in front of them. Tell the children to gather the string in their hands. Have the children listen to your words and follow your actions. Say:

> *The shepherd came in through the gate, and the sheep listened to his voice.* (Make the sheep wiggle by moving the string.)
> *The shepherd called the sheep by name.* (Say, "Hello, [name of sheep]!")
> *Then the shepherd led the sheep out of the pen.* (Walk two steps, and pull the sheep with you.)

Then the shepherd went ahead of the sheep (walk away from the sheep, and let out the string)

Until the shepherd was far, far away. (Wave to the sheep that's far, far away.)

But the sheep followed him because he is their shepherd and they knew his voice. (Start pulling the sheep toward you, gathering the string in your hand.)

The sheep followed until they were very, very near the shepherd. (Stop pulling when the sheep is by your feet again.)

The shepherd cared for his sheep, and he loved them.

After you've acted out the story, play a game of Tag. Have the children walk around the room, pulling their sheep. Designate one area of the room as a sheepfold. Act as the shepherd: As you tag each child, have him or her take his sheep to the sheepfold.

Be sure to send the shepherd's sheep home along with copies of the Direction Box.

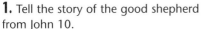
Extension Idea

● Make a snack any sheep would love: green pastures and quiet waters. Tint coconut green by adding a few drops of green food coloring to coconut in a plastic bag. Shake until the color is evenly distrib-uted. Tint white frosting blue with food coloring. Spread the blue frosting on a sugar cookie to create the quiet waters. Sprinkle the green coconut around the water to create the green pastures.

CRAFT SUMMARY:
Create construction paper animal puppets that help praise the Lord.

LEARNING GOAL:
To recognize shapes and animal sounds

LESSON CONNECTION:
Use this idea when children are learning about praising God.

SPRINKLING OF SUPPLIES:
You'll need glue sticks, craft sticks, construction paper, scissors, and markers.

PRIOR PREP:
Using several colors of construction paper, cut out several small and large triangles, circles, squares, and ovals for each child.
Photocopy the Direction Box from the next page for each child.

Animals Praise God

CREATING THE CRAFT

Craft Time:
15 min.

Invite children to make bears, birds, fish, and other animals using the construction paper shapes. Show children how to start with a large shape and glue smaller shapes to the large shapes to represent ears, eyes, noses, or fins. For example, to make a bear, begin with a large circle. Glue small circles at the top for ears and a triangle for a nose. Add other facial features with a marker.

When the animals are finished, show the children how to glue craft sticks to the backs of the animals to create puppets. As the children are working, ask them what animals they're making. Talk about what those animals do and what sounds they make. For example, if a child is making a bear, explain that bears growl and eat berries and fish.

When children have finished making the animal puppets, play the following learning game together.

PLAYING THE GAME

Game Time:
10 min.

Have the children sit in a circle with their puppets. Say: **Let's play a game about praising God. First listen to what the Bible says about who can praise God.** Read aloud Psalm 150:6: **"Let everything that has breath praise the Lord."** Ask:

● **What kinds of things breathe?**

Help the children discover that people and animals breathe—even fish breathe.

To play the game, read the Bible verse out loud and then call out the name of an animal. Have children who made that animal praise God using the sounds that animal makes. Repeat until you've mentioned each animal the children have made. End the game by saying: **"Let everything that has breath praise the Lord." Let all the children praise the Lord.**

Be sure to send the animal puppets home along with copies of the Direction Box.

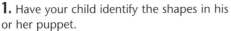
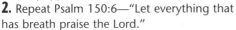
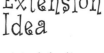

Extension Idea

● Instead of making construction paper puppets, use tongue depressors, craft sticks, pretzel sticks, and different sizes of Styrofoam balls to make three-dimensional puppets of each animal. For instance, a large Styrofoam ball could be attached to a small ball with pretzel sticks, creating the head and body of a bear. Then other small balls could be attached for the legs.

Sock Snowmen

CREATING THE CRAFT

Craft Time:
15 min.

Give each child a tube sock and three rubber bands. Set out the rest of the supplies. First have the children stuff their socks with fiberfill, leaving two or three inches at the top. Using the rubber bands, help children section the tube sock into three parts. Put the largest section at the toe end, then make a medium-sized section, and end with the smallest section. Leave two to three inches at the top.

Show the children how to roll the last three inches down to make a hat. Have the children use markers to draw on a face. If you want, children may tie scraps of fabric around their snowmen's "necks" as scarves. Children may also glue rectangular sections of black felt to the tops of their snowmen to form crowns for the hats; the rolled portions of the socks form the brims. Be sure to write each child's name on his or her snowman.

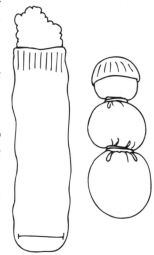

When children have finished making the sock snowmen, play the following learning game together.

PLAYING THE GAME

Game Time:
10 min.

Set up three sizes of bowls (small, medium, and large) for the children to toss their snowmen into. Position the bowls in a line so they form a snowman shape. Have the children take turns tossing their snowmen into the bowls. When a snowman lands, have the children identify whether it landed in the small bowl, the medium bowl, or the large bowl. Children can also practice aiming for a particular size of bowl.

Older preschoolers will enjoy keeping score for themselves. Give children pieces of paper and pens, and show them how to make hatch marks. If their snowmen land in the largest bowl, they earn one point. If their snowmen land in the medium-sized bowl, they earn two points. And if their snowmen land in the smallest bowl, they earn three points. At the end of the game, have each child count up all of his or her hatch marks. Don't compare scores or declare a winner—just use the game as a chance to practice new skills.

Be sure to send the sock snowmen home along with copies of the Direction Box.

Sock Snowmen

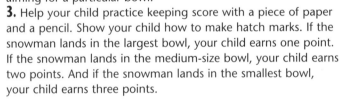

OBJECT: To understand the concepts of counting; simple addition; and small, medium, and large

1. Set out three bowls—a small, a medium, and a large—in a snowman shape.

2. Have your child toss the sock snowman into one of the bowls and identify whether it landed in the small, medium, or large bowl. Your child can also practice aiming for a particular bowl.

3. Help your child practice keeping score with a piece of paper and a pencil. Show your child how to make hatch marks. If the snowman lands in the largest bowl, your child earns one point. If the snowman lands in the medium-size bowl, your child earns two points. And if the snowman lands in the smallest bowl, your child earns three points.

Permission to photocopy this box from *More Than Mud Pies* granted for local church use.
Copyright © Group Publishing, Inc., P.O. Box 481, Loveland, CO 80539.

Extension Ideas

● Have children make and eat marshmallow snowmen. Show children how to stack three marshmallows on top of each other and use white frosting between them for the glue. Use M&M's candies for eyes, black licorice for a hat, and red rope licorice for a scarf.

● Make snow ice cream. If you live in an area with clean snow, fill a large mixing bowl with snow, and mix the snow with one can of sweetened condensed milk and a tablespoon of vanilla extract. Be sure to fold the mixture gently so it stays fluffy. Serve immediately.

CRAFT SUMMARY:
Make colorful bugs for an
"all-around" great game.

LEARNING GOAL:
To practice descriptive language and observation

LESSON CONNECTION:
Use this idea when children
are learning about the plague
of locusts.

SPRINKLING OF
SUPPLIES:
You'll need scissors, construction paper, pipe cleaners,
plastic bags, crayons or markers, and a hole punch.

PRIOR PREP:
Cut red, yellow, and blue construction paper into six-inch
circles, squares, and triangles.
You'll need one of each shape
for each child. In each shape,
punch two holes about two
inches away from each other.
Photocopy the Direction Box
from the next page for each
child.

Bags-o-Bugs

CREATING THE CRAFT

Craft Time: 10 min.

Set out the pipe cleaners and the crayons or markers. Hand each child a circle, a square, and a triangle. Have the children use crayons or markers to draw eyes on the shapes and further decorate them to look like bugs. Then have each child thread two pipe cleaners up from the bottom of each bug, through one hole, and down through the second hole so both ends of the pipe cleaners are on the bottom side of the bug. Show children how to bend both ends of the pipe cleaners out to form legs. Have the children follow the same procedure for all three of their shapes so they have three bugs. If you'd like the children to make bugs that are a little bit more realistic, have them add pipe cleaners to make six- or eight-legged bugs. Have each child put all three of his or her bugs into a plastic bag.

When children have finished making the bags-o-bugs, play the following learning game together.

PLAYING THE GAME

Game Time: 10 min.

Have children sit in a circle and put their bags-o-bugs in front of them. Say: **When I close my eyes, choose one of your bugs and put it somewhere on your body.** Shut your eyes, and sing these lines to the tune of "Twinkle, Twinkle, Little Star":

Over, under, on, around:
Where's the little bug to be found?

You can sing the same two lines all the way through the tune of the song. When you're finished singing, open your eyes and describe where one of the bugs is. For exam-ple, if Christopher put his red triangle bug under his knee, you'd say: **I spy a red triangle bug under someone's knee.** Have the children look around until they discover that you've spied Christopher's bug. After a few rounds, let the children take turns shutting their eyes and describing where a bug is.

You can also use the bugs to practice color and shape concepts. Have children sit in a circle, and have each child hold a bug. Start walking around the circle to the left, and have the children pass the bugs to their right. Then stop walking, and have children hold the bugs they have. Have the children take turns describing the bugs they're holding—for example, "I have a yellow triangle bug" or "I have a red square bug."

Be sure to send the bags-o-bugs home along with copies of the Direction Box.

Extension Idea

● For tasty bugs, have the children spread colored cream cheese on round, square, or triangle crackers. Show children how to drape short sections of cooked spaghetti in the middle of the crackers for legs and then add another cracker on top. Use two dots of cream cheese for eyes. You could also use frosting and skinny licorice. Chow down on your crunchy bugs! Yum!

Bags-o-Bugs

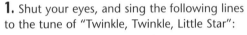

OBJECT: To practice descriptive language and observation

1. Shut your eyes, and sing the following lines to the tune of "Twinkle, Twinkle, Little Star":

> *Over, under, on, around:*
> *Where's the little bug to be found?*

2. As you sing, have your child take all three bugs and place them over, under, on, or around something in the room. Have your child put each bug in a different place.

3. Open your eyes, and hunt for the bugs. When you've found one, say, for example, "I spy a blue square bug on the table."

4. Have your child run to that bug and bring it to you.

5. Repeat the process for the other two bugs.

6. Then have your child take a turn closing his or her eyes while you place the bugs around the room.

LEARNING GOAL:
To recognize the sounds of letters and to practice fine motor skills

LESSON CONNECTION:
Use this idea when children are learning about hiding God's Word in their hearts (Psalm 119:11).

SPRINKLING OF SUPPLIES:
You'll need instant vanilla pudding mix, quart-sized resealable freezer bags, milk, measuring cups and spoons, plastic spoons, food coloring, and a wet washrag.

PRIOR PREP:
Photocopy the Direction Box from the next page for each child.

Scribes' Tablets

CREATING THE CRAFT

Craft Time: 10 min.

Give each child a resealable freezer bag. Into each bag, pour one-fourth cup of milk and two tablespoons of instant vanilla pudding mix. Release the excess air in the bags, and seal them; then wipe them off with the washrag if anything has spilled on the outside. Have the children knead their bags to mix the ingredients. The pudding will quickly get thick to create "scribes' tablets."

When children have finished making the scribes' tablets, play the following learning game together.

PLAYING THE GAME

Game Time: 15 min.

Have the children sit in a circle on the floor, setting their scribes' tablets in front of them. Direct the children to spread the pudding inside the bag so it forms a flat, even layer. Call out letters, and have the children write the letters on the tablets with their fingers. Help children who don't know how to form certain letters. In between letters, have the children "erase" the tablets by gently spreading the pudding flat again.

With older preschoolers, call out words and have children write down the letter each word starts with. Older preschoolers can also put several scribes' tablets in a row to practice writing simple words such as "cat" and "dog."

Have the children put one letter on each tablet. Then help them sound out the words.

To end the game, give each child a spoon, and let children open their bags and eat the contents of their tablets.

You can also use this activity to help children practice color skills. Add a drop of food coloring to the pudding in each bag. Have the children find an object in the room that matches the color of their pudding.

Be sure to send copies of the Direction Box home with the children.

Extension Ideas

● Use the scribes' tablets with the same learning game to help children work on number skills.

● Have each child draw a letter and a number on a friend's back. Have the friend guess what the letter or number is.

Scribes' Tablets

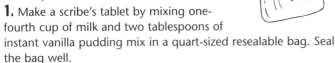

OBJECT: To recognize the sounds of letters and to practice fine motor skills

1. Make a scribe's tablet by mixing one-fourth cup of milk and two tablespoons of instant vanilla pudding mix in a quart-sized resealable bag. Seal the bag well.

2. Have your child lay the tablet flat on a table and spread the pudding evenly within the bag. Call out letters, and have your child write them on the pudding with his or her finger.

3. Then call out words, and have your child write the letter each word starts with.

4. When you're finished, let your child open the bag and eat the tablet with a spoon.

CRAFT SUMMARY:
Create decorative cartons for
a letter game.

LEARNING GOAL:
To recognize letters and
sounds

LESSON CONNECTION:
Use this idea when children
are learning about Creation.

**SPRINKLING OF
SUPPLIES:**
You'll need an empty egg carton and a small marshmallow
for each child; extra marshmallows for children to
munch on; and colorful markers, glue sticks, construction
paper, letter stickers, and
happy-face stickers.

PRIOR PREP:
Photocopy the Direction Box
from the next page for each
child.

Shake, Rattle, and Roll

CREATING THE CRAFT

Craft Time:
15 min.

Set out the markers, glue sticks, and construction paper. Give each child an empty egg
carton and a copy of the Direction Box. Help the children
glue a Direction Box to the top of each carton. Then have
the children decorate the outsides of their cartons with the
construction paper. For fun, have children tear off sections
of paper and curl the sections around markers before they
glue the sections to the cartons. You could also provide a
hole punch so the children could make confetti. This is
also a great way to use up craft scraps such as feathers,
stickers, and ribbon.

When children have decorated their cartons, have the
children open the cartons and put letter stickers in half of the
egg cups. Give children stickers of letters with strong consonant sounds—b, t, and s, for
example. Then have chil-
dren put happy-face stickers
in the other egg cups.

When children have
finished making these "egg-
stra"-special egg cartons,
play the following learning
game together.

PLAYING THE GAME

Game Time:
10 min.

Hand each child a small "game marshmallow" to place in their egg cartons. Explain that
the game is called Shake, Rattle, and Roll because children

will shake their egg cartons to play. Show the children how to shake an egg carton. As you shake the carton, say: **Shake, shake, shake—what letter did I make?**

Open the carton, and see where the marshmallow landed. If it landed on a letter, have the children identify the letter and say the sound the letter makes. Have the children name something God made that starts with that letter. If the marshmallow landed on a happy face, have the children exchange high fives and say, "God made everything."

Have the children form pairs and play the game together. Let them continue playing for several more shakes, rattles, and rolls. Then hand each child several fresh marshmallows to munch.

Be sure to send the decorated egg cartons with stickers inside home with the children.

Extension Ideas

● Shake, rattle, and roll; then identify an object in the room that begins with the same letter or sound as the letter the marshmallow landed on.

● Provide a bowl of alphabet cereal or noodles, and invite the children to find letters that match the ones in their egg cups. Place the cereal bits or noodles in the appropriate cups.

Shake, Rattle, and Roll

OBJECT: To recognize letters and sounds

1. Place a small "game marshmallow" in the carton, and close the lid.

2. Shake the carton as you say, "Shake, shake, shake—what letter did I make?"

3. Open the carton, and note where the marshmallow landed. If it's on a letter, identify the letter and the sound that letter makes. Name something God made that starts with that letter. If the marshmallow landed on a happy face, exchange a high five with your partner and say, "God made everything."

4. Take turns playing the game.

CRAFT SUMMARY:
Make cardboard wheels with
letters of the alphabet.

LEARNING GOAL:
To identify letters of the
alphabet

LESSON CONNECTION:
Use this idea when children
are learning about God's love
for people.

SPRINKLING OF
SUPPLIES:
You'll need paper, paper plates,
a ruler, markers or crayons,
scissors, glue, a sharp pencil,
and paper fasteners.

PRIOR PREP:
On a sheet of paper, draw a
circle that's the same size as
the flat, interior section of the
paper plates you're using. Use
a ruler to divide this circle into
eight to sixteen pie wedges.
Near the edge of the circle in
each wedge, draw a different
letter of the alphabet. Use letters with strong consonant
sounds rather than vowels.
Photocopy this circle for each
child.
For each child, make another
circle the same size but without the letters or the pie-
shaped wedges. From the
edge of each of these circles,
cut out a section of the circle
to create a letter window (see
illustration). Photocopy the
Direction Box from the next
page for each child.

Alphabet Wheels

CREATING THE CRAFT

Craft
Time:
10 min.

Have each child glue an alphabet circle to the center of a paper plate. While the glue is drying, have the children color the second paper circle with markers or crayons. Then have the children put their decorated circles on top of their alphabet circles. Carefully use a sharp pencil to poke a hole through the center of each circle; then put the pencil away so children won't hurt themselves. Then have the children use paper fasteners to connect their letter windows to their alphabet circles. Children should be able to hold their alphabet wheels with one hand and use the other hand to turn the top letter window around to reveal different letters of the alphabet.

When children have finished making the alphabet wheels, play the following learning game together.

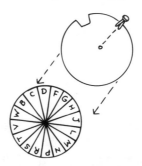

PLAYING THE GAME

Game
Time:
10 min.

Have the children turn the letter windows of their alphabet wheels while they say this rhyme:

A, B, C, D, E, F, G.
Letters are such fun, you see.
The alphabet wheel will soon reveal
That next will be the letter ___.

Have the children stop turning their wheels and see what letter is showing in the window. Have the children identify the letter and think of a person's name that begins with that letter.

End the game with a prayer, thanking God for the people children mentioned during the game and for creating people.

Be sure to send the alphabet wheels home along with copies of the Direction Box.

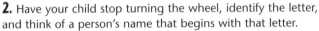

Alphabet Wheels

OBJECT: To identify letters of the alphabet

1. Have your child turn the wheel while you say this rhyme:

A, B, C, D, E, F, G.
Letters are such fun, you see.
The alphabet wheel will soon reveal
That next will be the letter ___.

2. Have your child stop turning the wheel, identify the letter, and think of a person's name that begins with that letter.

3. Write these letters on a piece of paper: __AT. Help your child see how the word changes when you put different letters at the beginning of it.

Story Starters

CREATING THE CRAFT

Craft Time: 15 min.

Have the children choose pictures they like and then glue them to index cards. Each child will need ten to fifteen cards. Help the children choose a variety of pictures including people, animals, plants, toys, buildings, and food. Children can also choose pictures of fun things to do, such as swimming, playing games, or riding rides at a carnival. Write the children's names on the backs of their cards. If you have additional time, have the children use markers to decorate envelopes in which to keep their cards. Set the cards aside to dry before putting them in the envelopes.

When children have finished making the story starters, play the following learning game together.

PLAYING THE GAME

Game Time: 10 min.

Put several of the cards face down on the floor. Gather the children in a circle around the cards. Have each child choose a card and turn it over. Then tell a story together by going around the room and having each child say how the subject of his or her card is involved in the story. For example, if you turn over a card that shows a bird, you could start the story by saying, "This little bird was flying in the park one day. It saw a beautiful…" Then if the next child turned over a picture of a little boy, he or she could say, "…boy who was playing in the park."

Keep going around the circle even if the pictures don't really fit in the story. Once the children catch on, they'll tell a silly story about their pictures no matter what they are. The longer you play, the sillier the stories will be. When everyone has explained their cards' roles in the story, end the story with a completer sentence such as "And it was a lovely day" or "And they all had fun." Turn the cards over, reshuffle, and play again.

Use these story starters to help children apply the Bible. If your lesson is on being kind, have the children tell how the people or animals in the story starters showed kindness.

You can also use these story starters to play a memory game. Show the children three cards, and then place the cards face down on a table. Have the children see if they can remember where each picture is. Add cards for the next round. Continue until children can remember the positions of ten cards.

Be sure to send the story starters home along with copies of the Direction Box.

Story Starters

OBJECT: To encourage storytelling and imagination

1. Turn the cards face down on a table, and mix them up.
2. Turn over five cards.
3. Together, tell a story about the pictures on the cards.
4. Turn the cards back over, reshuffle, and play again.

SECTION TWO:

Body Skills

CRAFT SUMMARY:
Create a pond of colorful fish.

LEARNING GOAL:
To develop eye-hand coordination and counting skills

LESSON CONNECTION:
Use this idea when children are learning about the disciples being fishers of men.

SPRINKLING OF SUPPLIES:
You'll need colorful construction paper, scissors, dot stickers in many colors, drinking straws, string, paper clips, tape, index cards, and markers or crayons. You'll also need a small magnet for each child. To provide these inexpensively, cut a vinyl refrigerator magnet into small pieces.

PRIOR PREP:
Cut out three fish shapes from construction paper and a two-foot piece of string for each child.
Photocopy the Direction Box from the next page for each child.

Counting Fish

CREATING THE CRAFT

Craft Time: 15 min.

Have each child decorate three paper fish with markers or crayons and the dot stickers. Have younger preschoolers use no more than five dots per fish. Older preschoolers may use up to ten dots per fish. Also make sure that the children put a different number of dots on each fish. Help the children write their names on the backs of their fish. Then help the children slide a paper clip onto each fish.

To make fishing poles, give each child a straw and piece of string. Help each child tape the string to the straw and then tape a magnet to the other end of the string.

When children have finished making the counting fish and the fishing poles, play the following learning game together.

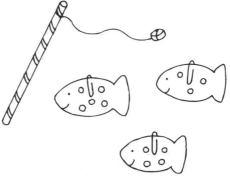

PLAYING THE GAME

Game Time: 15 min.

Put a piece of string on the floor in a circle to form a pond. Put all the fish on the floor in the pond. Have the children sit in a circle two feet back from the fish pond. Have the children keep their fishing poles in their laps.

Have one child at a time "fish" by lowering his or her pole over the pond until the magnet picks up a fish. Have the child count the dots on the fish. Then lead all the children in counting up to that number. Make sure every child gets a chance to fish and count.

Then try this variation. As the children catch fish, call out different colors of dot stickers, and have the children count the amount of dots for each color. Then have children clap once for each dot they counted. For example, if children counted three red dots, have them clap three times. Try hopping for the blue dots, turning in circles for the yellow dots, and so forth.

Another way to increase the learning is to write numbers on index cards, and set them out in order on a table. Have each child catch a fish, count the dots on the fish, and match it to a number card.

Be sure to send the counting fish and fishing poles home along with copies of the Direction Box.

Counting Fish

OBJECT: To develop eye-hand coordination and counting skills

1. Place the fish on the floor.
2. Use the magnet on the fishing pole to catch a fish.
3. Count the dots on the fish out loud.
4. Try catching each of the fish several times.

CRAFT SUMMARY:
Fill and decorate mini-maracas.

LEARNING GOAL:
To encourage musical rhythm and beat

LESSON CONNECTION:
Use this idea when children are learning about Palm Sunday or about praising God.

SPRINKLING OF SUPPLIES:
You'll need one or two plastic eggs per child; small stickers; tape; bowls of filler such as beans, rice, or beads; small scoops such as quarter-cup measuring cups or detergent scoops; and a permanent marker. You'll also need an audiocassette player or CD player and tapes or CDs in several musical styles.

PRIOR PREP:
Photocopy the Direction Box from the next page for each child.

Melodious Mini-Maracas

CREATING THE CRAFT

Craft Time: 15 min.

Set out the small scoops and bowls of filler such as beans, rice, or beads. Have the children separate their eggs and carefully put one scoop of filler material into one half of each egg. Have the children close the eggs, and help them tape the eggs shut. Then have the children decorate the eggs with stickers. While the children are decorating, tell them that God loves to hear us make joyful noises to him. Talk about what kinds of joyful noises children can make for God. Be sure to write children's names on their eggs with the permanent marker.

When children have finished making the melodious mini-maracas, play the following learning game together.

PLAYING THE GAME

Game Time: 10 min.

Have the children gather in a circle. Start saying: **Jesus** and shaking your mini-maracas on each syllable of the word. Have the children repeat your words and actions. Then try: **Jesus loves me** and **Jesus loves** (your own name). Try several other words that have to do with praising God.

Then try shaking the mini-maracas to the beat of a song. Start by shaking the maracas while you sing "Jesus Loves Me." Then try shaking along to the beat as you play recordings of music. Try fast songs and slow songs. For a challenge, shake along with classical music such as the *Nutcracker Suite* or Vivaldi's *Four Seasons*.

Try these fun game variations:

● Pair up the children, and have them mimic each other's rhythms.

● Have the children shake their maracas while they march in a parade around the room.

● See what other sounds children can make with the maracas. Tap the maracas against children's hands like tambourines. Tap the maracas against the ground. Tap the maracas against each other.

Be sure to send the melodious mini-maracas home along with copies of the Direction Box.

Melodious Mini-Maracas

OBJECT: To encourage musical rhythm and beat

1. Use the maracas to shake out the syllables of words. Try names of people in the family, names for God, the name "Jesus," the words "Jesus loves me," or the words "Jesus loves (fill in names)."

2. Now try shaking the mini-maracas to the beat of a song. Start with the song "Jesus Loves Me." Try fast songs and slow songs.

3. For a challenge, shake along with classical music such as the *Nutcracker Suite* or Vivaldi's *Four Seasons.*

Decorate coffee filters to make rainbow parachutes.

LEARNING GOAL:
To develop eye-hand coordination and large motor skills

LESSON CONNECTION:
Use this activity when children are learning about Noah.

SPRINKLING OF SUPPLIES:
You'll need a crayon for each student, scissors, newspaper, coffee filters, liquid food coloring, a permanent marker, a hole punch, tape or chalk, boxes, rope, rubbing alcohol, eyedroppers, and string.

PRIOR PREP:
For each student, cut four twelve-inch lengths of string. Then tie all four lengths of string to a crayon. Also punch four evenly spaced holes around the edge of each coffee filter (at 3 o'clock, 6 o'clock, 9 o'clock, and 12 o'clock).
Photocopy the Direction Box from the next page for each child.

Rainbow Parachutes

CREATING THE CRAFT

Craft Time:
10 min.

Cover the art area with several layers of newspaper. Set out coffee filters and bottles of liquid food coloring. Write each child's name on a coffee filter with a permanent marker. Have the children spread out their coffee filters as flat as possible and use the food coloring to drip the colors of their choice onto the filters. It should only take four or five drops of food coloring to color the filters. The liquid will saturate the filter and make a beautiful blending of colors. Set the filters aside to dry on more layers of newspaper.

TEACHER TIP

You may want to use paint smocks for this activity. If you don't have paint smocks, you can roll up children's sleeves and then fasten old towels around children's torsos with large binder clips.

If you add some rubbing alcohol to each color, the colors will dry faster and will be more vibrant on the coffee filter. To do this, squeeze out the food coloring into small bowls, and add a teaspoon of rubbing alcohol. Provide eye droppers, or pour the coloring back into the bottles. Be sure not to use this coloring for future food projects.

When the filters are dry, help children tie the crayons to the filters by threading the four strings through the four holes in the filter and tying knots.

When children have finished making the rainbow parachutes, play the following learning game together.

Game Time: 10 min.

Use tape or chalk to mark a large circle for the children to stand around. Set out boxes, or mark smaller circles within the big circle to be targets for the parachutes to land in. You may also want to string a rope across the room about a foot higher than children can reach.

Gather the children around the circle, and say: **The Bible tells us that once the entire world was flooded. Noah, his family, and all the animals lived on a boat because there was no dry land anywhere. When the flood finally went away, Noah, his family, and all the animals came out of the ark onto dry land. God put a rainbow in the sky to remind them of his promise never to send a flood like that again. We're going to send our rainbow parachutes into the sky and watch them land.**

Have the children throw their parachutes into the air and watch them land. Have children try to get the parachutes to land in the boxes. Also have children fly their parachutes over the rope. Play for several minutes.

Be sure to send the rainbow parachutes home along with copies of the Direction Box.

Extension Ideas

● Use tape or chalk to make two parallel lines as a "river." Have the children take their parachutes and line up two by two (as the animals lined up to go onto the ark) across the river from each other. Encourage children to try to make their parachutes land near their partners on the other side of the river.

● To encourage color recognition, point to a color on each child's rainbow parachute, and ask the child to identify what color you are pointing to.

Rainbow Parachutes

OBJECT: To develop eye-hand coordination and large motor skills

1. Review the story of Noah and the rainbow that God put in the sky.

2. Have your child throw his or her rainbow parachute up into the air and watch where it lands.

3. Set out a box or create a masking tape circle, and have your child try to get the parachute to land in the box or circle.

4. Play catch with the parachute.

CRAFT SUMMARY:
Create reflecting stars.

LEARNING GOAL:
To develop coordination

LESSON CONNECTION:
Use this idea when children are learning about Esther, whose name is similar to the Persian word for "star." You can also use this activity when children are learning about Philippians 2:14-16.

SPRINKLING OF SUPPLIES:
You'll need poster board, a marker, scissors, star fruit, and aluminum foil.

PRIOR PREP:
Draw two stars for each child on the poster board, and cut the stars out. Older preschoolers may be able to cut the stars out themselves. You may also want to provide glue sticks and metallic glitter. Photocopy the Direction Box from the next page for each child.

Shining Stars

CREATING THE CRAFT

Craft Time: 10 min.

The game works best on a sunny day.

Have each child make two shining stars. Set out the poster board stars, scissors, and large pieces of aluminum foil. Have the children take each star and cover it with aluminum foil. Help the children cut the foil in between the stars' points and wrap the foil behind the points. Children may want to glue metallic glitter to their stars. Have them rub the foil with a glue stick and sprinkle on the glitter. Set the stars aside to dry.

When children have finished making the shining stars, play the following learning game together.

PLAYING THE GAME

Game Time: 10 min.

Say: **The Bible** (Philippians 2:15) **says we can shine like stars. Let's make our stars shine by reflecting the sunlight onto a wall.**

Show the children how to "catch" the sunlight and reflect it onto a wall. Have the children make their spots of sunlight dance on the wall while you sing the following song to the tune of "Twinkle, Twinkle, Little Star":

Twinkle, twinkle, little star.
God has sent you from afar
Into a world so dark and dim
To shine the love that comes from him.
Twinkle, twinkle, little star.
God has sent you from afar.

After you sing the song, point to the light on the wall that's from your star. Sing the song again, and have the children move their lights in the same way that you move yours. For example, on the first line of the song, bounce

40

your light to the right. On line two, bounce it to the left. On line three, bounce down. On line four, bounce up. On line five, bounce right. And on line six, bounce left. Then let the children take turns leading the class.

While the children are reflecting the sunlight on the wall, have them take turns moving their light on the wall and telling how they can shine for Jesus. Then, enjoy a "starry" snack with your children. Cut up star fruit, and let the children eat it.

Be sure to send the shining stars home along with copies of the Direction Box.

Shining Stars

OBJECT: To develop coordination

1. Read Philippians 2:15 together. Find some sunlight, and use the star to reflect the sunlight onto a wall.

2. Make the light bounce while you sing the following song to the tune of "Twinkle, Twinkle, Little Star." Have your child make his or her light bounce along with yours.

> *Twinkle, twinkle, little star.*
> *God has sent you from afar*
> *Into a world so dark and dim*
> *To shine the love that comes from him.*
> *Twinkle, twinkle, little star.*
> *God has sent you from afar.*

3. The second time through the song, follow your child's light movements on the wall.

CRAFT SUMMARY:
Create wooden instruments.

LEARNING GOAL:
To practice rhythm and
sequential memory

LESSON CONNECTION:
Use this idea when children
are learning about King David
and the ark of the covenant in
2 Samuel 6.

**SPRINKLING OF
SUPPLIES:**
You'll need two six-inch-long,
half-inch-diameter dowels for
each child and washable
markers.

PRIOR PREP:
Photocopy the Direction Box
from the next page for each
child.

Echo Sticks

CREATING THE CRAFT

Craft Time:
10 min.

Set out the markers and dowels. Have the children use the markers to decorate their echo sticks with colorful designs and patterns.

When children have finished making the echo sticks, play the following learning game together.

PLAYING THE GAME

Game Time:
15 min.

Throughout this activity, instruct the children to never tap their sticks on furniture or people; the sticks should only be tapped with other sticks. Say: **King David and the people in his kingdom were celebrating. They were happy because they knew God was with them. We can celebrate too! Let's imagine that we're a marching band. Marching bands are in parades to celebrate special events.**

Have the children line up for a parade. Tell the children to "follow the leader" and tap their sticks the same way you do. Also tell the children that when you want them to listen, you'll hold the sticks up in the air. Take the lead, and begin tapping out a simple rhythm with your sticks. To begin, tap the sticks each time you take a step. Have the children follow your beat.

When they have caught on to the concept, change the rhythm to double beats or triple beats while you march. Older preschoolers will enjoy taking the lead and picking a rhythm for the other children to copy.

For more fun, play praise music and tap the sticks to the rhythm of music as King David did.

Tap out the rhythm of each child's first and last name. Try tapping out the rhythm of the words Jerusalem, Israelites, David, and Mephibosheth (muh-FIB-uh-sheth).

Be sure to send the echo sticks home along with copies of the Direction Box.

Echo Sticks

OBJECT: To practice rhythm and sequential memory

1. Clap a simple rhythm.

2. Have your child repeat the rhythm by tapping the echo sticks together.

3. Then have your child tap out a rhythm.

4. Repeat the rhythm by clapping it.

5. Read about a celebration in Psalm 150.

SPRINKLING OF SUPPLIES:

You'll need two sturdy paper plates for each child; a hole punch; scissors; yarn; dry beans; transparent tape; a small scoop; and any combination of crayons, washable markers, bingo daubers, and stickers to decorate the tambourines.

PRIOR PREP:

Put two paper plates together—don't "nest" the plates, but position them so there's an open space between them. Punch about twelve holes through the edges of the plates, being sure to punch through both paper plates. Make a punched set of paper plates for each child. Photocopy the Direction Box from the next page for each child.

Trusty Tambourines

CREATING THE CRAFT

Craft Time:
15 min.

Set out the crayons, markers, bingo daubers, stickers, and any other items children can use to decorate the paper plates. Encourage the children to decorate their plates in any way they wish using the supplies on hand.

While children are working, cut a three-foot length of yarn for each child. Tightly tape one end of each piece of yarn to make a "needle" the child can use to lace together the plates. Tape the other end of the yarn to the back side of one plate so the yarn won't pull through when the child laces. Put a small scoop of dry beans on one of each child's plates.

Have children place the second plate on top of the plate containing the beans and then line up the holes. Tape the plates together to hold the beans inside. Help the children lace the plates together. When children have gone around the plates with lacing, pull the yarn tightly and tie it off.

When children have finished making the trusty tambourines, play the following learning game together.

PLAYING THE GAME

Game Time:
10 min.

Have the children hold their trusty tambourines and stand in a circle. Repeat the following rhyme, and have each child take a turn moving so his or her tambourine makes noise.

My tambourine's trusty! It's easy to prove:
It always makes noise when I do this move.

Here are some examples of different movements children can do:

- Jump up and down.
- Shake the tambourine.
- Tap the tambourine with your hand.
- Slide the tambourine back and forth.
- Do the twist.
- Holding the tambourine still, bend quickly from the waist.
- Move the tambourine in an arc over your head.
- Twirl around.
- Slide the tambourine on the floor.
- Toss the tambourine and catch it.

To end the game and lead the children into a more quiet activity, say the following rhyme:

My tambourine's trusty! It's been lots of fun,
But now it's time for quiet since the game is done.

Be sure to send the trusty tambourines home along with copies of the Direction Box.

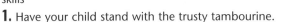
Extension Ideas

- Have the children string jingle bells onto the tambourines while they're lacing the plates together.

- Have the children toss the tambourines like Frisbee discs, run to where they land, and then toss them again.

Cup-Catch Game

CREATING THE CRAFT

Craft Time: 15 min.

Give each child a disposable cup and a piece of paper to crumple into a ball. Then have the children decorate their cups with markers. While the children are working, thread a two-foot length of string through the hole of each child's cup, and secure the string by making a large knot on the inside of the cup. Cover the hole with a piece of tape to keep the knot from pulling through. Use a sharp needle with a large eye to thread the other end of the string through the paper ball; then tie a knot so the string doesn't pull through. If you'd rather not use the needle, you can simply tie the string around the paper ball.

When children have finished making the catch cups, play the following learning game together.

PLAYING THE GAME

Game Time: 10 min.

Tell children to pretend that the cup is God's hand and the ball is the world. Have children put the balls inside the cups and sing "He's Got the Whole World in His Hands." Then play the game together.

If you have young preschoolers, have them kneel next to a table and hold their cups close to the edge of the table with one hand as if they were going to take a drink from the cups. Have children use their other hands to put the paper balls on the table as far away from themselves as the strings will allow. Have the children slowly lower the cups, dragging the balls across the table until they fall off. Have children catch the balls in the cups. Each time a ball lands in a cup, have the child name someone God takes care of or a way God takes care of people.

If you have older children, have them hold the cups with the balls dangling by the strings. Tell children to gently toss the balls up in the air so they come down into the cups. Have children count how many times they can catch their balls in their cups.

Use the cup-catch craft as a creative movement tool. Play praise music. Have the children hold the cups and swing the paper balls in circles over their heads, to the left, and to the right.

Be sure to send the catch cups home along with copies of the Direction Box.

Extension Idea

● Play catch with other balls. Try Nerf balls, beach balls, and tennis balls. Practice rolling, tossing, and bouncing the balls.

Cup-Catch Game

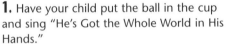

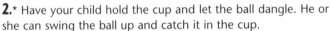

OBJECT: To improve manual dexterity and eye-hand coordination

1. Have your child put the ball in the cup and sing "He's Got the Whole World in His Hands."

2.* Have your child hold the cup and let the ball dangle. He or she can swing the ball up and catch it in the cup.

3. Each time your child catches the ball, have him or her name a person God cares for or a way God cares for people.

*Younger preschoolers can place the ball on a flat table and lower the cup, causing the ball to travel across the table, fall off the edge, and land in the cup.

Permission to photocopy this box from *More Than Mud Pies* granted for local church use.
Copyright © Group Publishing, Inc., P.O. Box 481, Loveland, CO 80539.

CRAFT SUMMARY:
Create scented clouds.

LEARNING GOAL:
To develop eye-hand coordination and understand the
concepts of up and down

LESSON CONNECTION:
Use this idea when children
are learning about Elijah and
the rain cloud from 1 Kings
18:41-45.

SPRINKLING OF
SUPPLIES:
You'll need scissors, fabric
softener sheets, pipe cleaners,
paper plates, cotton balls,
and markers or crayons.

PRIOR PREP:
Cut the pipe cleaners in half.
Photocopy the Direction Box
from the next page for each
child.

Light As a Cloud

CREATING THE CRAFT

Craft Time:
10 min.

Give each child a fabric softener sheet. Have each child put two or three cotton balls in the middle of the sheet. Then show the children how to gather up the edges of the fabric softener sheet and wrap the pipe cleaner around the edges, enclosing the cotton balls to create a sachet "cloud."

Give each child a paper plate. Set out markers or crayons, and have the children decorate their plates.

When children have finished making the clouds, play the following learning game together.

PLAYING THE GAME

Game Time:
15 min.

Gather the children in a circle. Tell the story of Elijah and the rain cloud from 1 Kings 18:41-45. Then say: **Let's watch our own rain clouds as they come close.** Have children set their clouds on their paper plates and then lift and lower their plates while you say this rhyme:

Up and down, up and down,
Softly, softly—don't touch the ground.

Say: **Let's toss our small clouds *up* in the air and catch them on our paper plates before they fall *down* to the ground.**

To toss the clouds, have the children hold on to their plates, use the plates to fling the clouds upward, and then try to catch the clouds as they fall back down. Have the children toss the clouds for several minutes.

Older children may enjoy tossing clouds back and forth with partners.

Be sure to send the clouds home along with copies of the Direction Box.

Extension Idea

● To make gifts, have children fill their clouds with rose petals or use drops of scented oil on cotton balls inside the sachet.

CREATING THE CRAFT

Craft Time: 10 min.

Set out the paper plates, crayons or markers, and scissors. Show children that the holes in the paper plates are "mouths." Have children use the crayons or markers to draw eyes and noses. They can use scissors to cut the tops of the paper plates into fringe that looks like hair. Have each child center his or her portrait on top of a bowl and tape the plates to the bowls.

When children are finished making feed-the-face bowls, play the following learning game together.

PLAYING THE GAME

Game Time: 10 min.

Spread out a clean, large tablecloth on the floor. Have the children put the feed-the-face bowls on the edge of the tablecloth. The children should stand off the tablecloth right next to their own bowls. Have the children spread out so there's plenty of space between them. Give each child a plastic bag of marshmallows. One by one, have the children drop their marshmallows into their feed-the-face bowls.

When each child has dropped all ten marshmallows, have the children gather the marshmallows that didn't make it inside the mouths into one pile. Then have children shake out all the marshmallows from their bowls and put them into another pile. Have the children count how many marshmallows went into the bowls. For each marshmallow that went in, have the children name a blessing they've received. Then have them count how many marshmallows didn't go into the bowls. Introduce older preschoolers to addition by explaining that the marshmallows that went in plus the marshmallows that didn't go in add up to ten marshmallows.

Have the children discover if the game is easier if they're sitting, kneeling, or standing next to their bowls.

Then sing this silly song to the tune of "Old MacDonald Had a Farm":

Our loving God gives us good food! Yes, he really does!
Vegetables, fruit, meats, and grains. My, it sure tastes
*   good.*
With a yum, yum, here and a slurp, slurp, there.
Here a munch, there a crunch.
Thank you, God, so very much!
Our loving God gives us good food! Yes, he really does!

Be sure to send the feed-the-face bowls home along with copies of the Direction Box.

Feed the Face

OBJECT: To develop coordination, counting, and simple addition

1. Have your child put the bowl on the floor and stand next to it.

2. Let your child try to drop ten marshmallows into the mouth.

3. Have your child pick up any marshmallows that are on the floor, put them in a pile, and count them.

4. Have your child shake out the marshmallows that went inside the mouth and count them. For each marshmallow, ask your child to name a blessing he or she has received.

5. Show your child that the marshmallows that went inside the mouth plus those that didn't go inside the mouth all add up to ten marshmallows.

6. Experiment with your child to discover whether the game is easier when he or she sits, kneels, or stands next to the feed-the-face bowl.

CRAFT SUMMARY:
Create candles to use in a fun jumping game.

LEARNING GOAL:
To develop large motor skills

LESSON CONNECTION:
Use this idea when children are learning that Jesus is the light of the world.

SPRINKLING OF SUPPLIES:
You'll need a paper towel tube for each child; red, yellow, and orange tissue paper; construction paper; glue; tape; and scissors.

PRIOR PREP:
Cut the construction paper to fit the length of a paper towel tube. The children will be rolling the paper around the tube, and it's OK if the paper overlaps.
Photocopy the Direction Box from the next page for each child.

Jack Be Nimble

CREATING THE CRAFT

Craft Time:
10 min.

Have each child use a glue stick or tacky craft glue to cover a cut sheet of construction paper with glue. Show children how to place a paper towel tube near one edge of the construction paper and roll the paper around the tube. Have the children carefully press the edge of the paper down. Set aside the tubes for a few minutes to let the glue dry.

While you're waiting, have the children tear the tissue paper into squares. Have children take at least three pieces of tissue in different colors and crumple and twist the pieces into a flame shape. Have the children tape their flames into the tops of their paper towel tubes.

When children have finished making the Jack-be-nimble candlesticks, play the following learning game together.

PLAYING THE GAME

Game Time:
10 min.

Have the children stand around the room with plenty of room between each other. Have them balance their candlesticks so they're standing on the floor. The ends may need to be trimmed with a pair of scissors to help the candlesticks stand upright. Encourage children to jump back and forth over their candlesticks while you say this rhyme:

Spotlight, starlight, sunlight, streetlight,
Jesus, you're the light of the world.
You're the brightest light, all right.

Teach the poem to the children, and have them practice saying it while they hop over their candlesticks.

For even more fun, line up all the children's candlesticks. Put about three feet of space between them. Then have the children line up and one by one walk the "obstacle course," jumping over each candlestick as they come to it.

Be sure to send the Jack-be-nimble candlesticks home along with copies of the Direction Box.

Extension Ideas

● Sing "This Little Light of Mine."

● Light a real candle, and say the poem as a prayer—reverently and quietly.

Jack Be Nimble

OBJECT: To develop large motor skills

1. Place the candlestick upright on the floor.

2. Encourage your child to jump back and forth over the candlestick.

3. Say this poem together:

> Spotlight, starlight, sunlight, streetlight,
> Jesus, you're the light of the world.
> You're the brightest light, all right.

Sensational Senses

CREATING THE CRAFT

Craft Time: 10 min.

Give each child two "Sensational Senses" handouts and ten index cards. Have the children cut out the pictures and glue them to the cards. Then have the children color the cards with markers or crayons.

When children have finished making the sensational senses cards, play the following learning game together.

PLAYING THE GAME

Game Time: 10 min.

Have everyone sit in a circle. Turn two sets of cards picture-side down on the floor. Have the children take turns turning two cards over. If the cards match, have the child say what the body part does. For example, if the child turns over two eyes, he or she would say that eyes see. Then have the child say something that eyes can see. For example, the child might say that eyes can see the blue sky.

If the cards don't match, have the child pick a silly action to do with the entire class. For example, children might jump up, twirl around, and sit back down.

Turn the cards back over, and give the next child a chance to turn two cards over. Play until everyone has had a chance to turn over two cards.

Older preschoolers may like to play this game with a partner.

For more fun, play this musical game. Turn the cards picture-side down. Turn one card over, and sing the following song with the verse that corresponds with the picture. Sing the song to the tune of "If You're Happy and You Know It."

Verse 1: *Put your finger on your ear; that's where you hear.* (Tap your ears.)
Put your finger on your ear; that's where you hear. (Tap your ears.)
Put your finger on your ear, put your finger on your ear.
Put your finger on your ear; that's where you hear. (Tap your ears.)

Verse 2: *Put your finger on your eye; that's where you see.* (Blink, blink.)

Verse 3: *Put your finger on your nose; that's where you smell.* (Sniff, sniff.)

Verse 4: *Put your finger on your finger; that's where you touch.* (Touch your fingers together.)

Verse 5: *Put your finger on your tongue; that's where you taste.* (Slurp, slurp.)

Be sure to send the sensational senses cards home along with copies of the Direction Box.

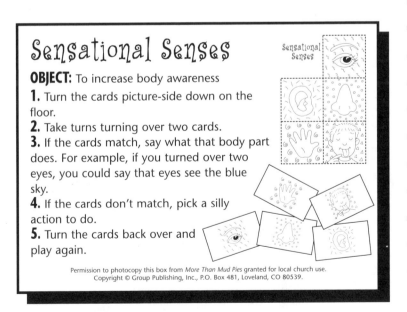

Sensational Senses

OBJECT: To increase body awareness
1. Turn the cards picture-side down on the floor.
2. Take turns turning over two cards.
3. If the cards match, say what that body part does. For example, if you turned over two eyes, you could say that eyes see the blue sky.
4. If the cards don't match, pick a silly action to do.
5. Turn the cards back over and play again.

Sensational Senses

SECTION THREE:

● ● ● ● ● ● ●

Thinking Skills

CRAFT SUMMARY:
Create caterpillars from fruit-flavored cereal.

LEARNING GOAL:
To understand color sorting and pattern identification

LESSON CONNECTION:
Use this idea when children are learning about following or obeying God.

SPRINKLING OF SUPPLIES:
You'll need fruit-flavored loop cereal, scissors, yarn, and paper plates.

PRIOR PREP:
Cut yarn into eighteen-inch lengths. Tie a piece of cereal at one end of each string. Photocopy the Direction Box from the next page for each child.

Fruity Caterpillars

CREATING THE CRAFT

Craft Time: 20 min.

Give each child a length of yarn and some cereal on a paper plate. Have children sort the cereal into separate piles by color. Show children how to string the cereal in a pattern to make pretty pretend caterpillars. Call out colors, and have the children string them in order. Older children will enjoy creating their own patterns. Have the children leave two or three inches at the end of their strings. When the children are finished, tie a piece of cereal at the end to finish off the caterpillars. If you have time, have the children make two caterpillars.

When children have finished making the fruity caterpillars, play the following learning game together.

PLAYING THE GAME

Game Time: 10 min.

Have the children sit in a circle with their caterpillars on their paper plates. To start the game, arrange your fruity caterpillar into a simple shape such as a circle. Have the children identify the shape and then arrange their caterpillars in the same shape. Then choose a volunteer to arrange his or her caterpillar in another shape, such as a square. Have all the children arrange their caterpillars in the same shape. Older children will enjoy shaping their caterpillars into more complex shapes or letters. Continue until everyone has had a chance to lead the game.

If you're using this activity during a lesson on obedience, explain that obeying God, parents, and teachers means following their important instructions just as children followed instructions when they made their caterpillars and when they followed the leader to arrange their caterpillars into shapes.

You can also call out numbers for the children to form or count out pieces of cereal to nibble on.

Another idea is to have the children form the letters in their names.

Be sure to send the fruity caterpillars home along with copies of the Direction Box.

Fruity Caterpillars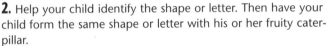

OBJECT: To understand color sorting and pattern identification

1. Arrange your caterpillar into a shape or a letter.

2. Help your child identify the shape or letter. Then have your child form the same shape or letter with his or her fruity caterpillar.

3. Next have your child arrange his or her caterpillar into a shape. Together, identify the shape or letter. Then arrange your own caterpillar into the same shape.

Crazy Creatures

CREATING THE CRAFT

Craft Time: 15 min.

Set out the nylons; tissue paper, toilet paper, or cotton batting; rubber bands; and markers.

Hand each child a nylon and some stuffing material. Help the children fill the nylon with stuffing and use the rubber bands to create legs, arms, noses, ears, and tails. If some children want floppy creatures, have them use less stuffing than they would for fully stuffed creatures.

When the animals are stuffed and the body parts are tied off, help the children use markers to create special features on their creatures. Help the children think of names for their crazy creatures, and write the names somewhere on the animals along with the children's names or initials.

When children have finished making the crazy creatures, play the following learning game together.

PLAYING THE GAME

Game Time: 10 min.

Have children stand in a circle, and ask children to hold up their crazy creatures. Say this rhyme:

Adam named the animals one by one.
It must have been a lot of fun.
Let's all play the same name game.
Tell us, what's your animal's name?

Have the first child to your left say the name of his or her animal. Say the rhyme again, and have the next child say what his or her animal's name is.

Continue around the circle until all the children have had the opportunity to introduce their crazy creatures. Encourage the children to learn the rhyme and say it with you as each child holds up his or her animal.

When all the crazy creatures have been introduced, say: **Let's play a game about all the special things your crazy creatures can do. Think of a special action your creature can do. For example, maybe your creature can hop or twirl or do a somersault. When it's your turn, say what your creature can do, and then we'll all do the action together.**

Start the game by holding up your animal and saying: **My creature can twirl.** Lead the children in twirling with their animals. Then have a volunteer call out what his or her animal can do. Have the child lead the other children in doing that action with their animals. Continue until everyone has a turn to lead.

Be sure to send the crazy creatures home along with copies of the Direction Box.

Extension Ideas

● Have the children tell about their creatures—what they eat, where they live, and the sounds they make.

● Encourage the children to tell good ways to care for their creatures. Have children act out the suggestions using their crazy creatures.

Crazy Creatures

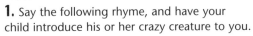

OBJECT: To encourage creative thinking and motor skills

1. Say the following rhyme, and have your child introduce his or her crazy creature to you.

> *Adam named the animals one by one.*
> *It must have been a lot of fun.*
> *Let's all play the same name game.*
> *Tell us, what's your animal's name?*

2. Have your child hold the creature and name an action it can do. For example, your child might say, "My creature can twirl."

3. Follow your child's action suggestion.

4. Then take a turn yourself by suggesting another action the creature can do, such as turn a somersault or do a deep knee-bend.

5. Continue taking turns.

Color Cups

CREATING THE CRAFT

Craft Time: 10 min.

Set out the paper cups and markers. Make sure each child has four cups. Encourage children to decorate their cups with the markers. Then write children's names or initials on the bottoms of their cups. After the children have decorated their cups, help children put one colored dot inside the bottom of each of their four cups. Have children use four different colors of stickers.

When children have finished making the color cups, play the following learning game together.

PLAYING THE GAME

Game Time: 10 min.

Have each child choose one of his or her four cups to begin the game. Have each child identify the color of the dot that's inside the cup. Then have children hunt for small items of the same color to fill the cup with. You may want to set out small toys and crayons for the children to put into the cups. Have children fill each of their cups with items the same color as the dot stickers. Then use the color cups for this fun game. Have the children sit in a circle. Then have them turn their cups upside down in front of them. When you say: **Pick a color,** have each child turn over one cup and identify the color. Have all the children who turned over a red-dotted cup do one jumping jack, those with yellow-dotted cups twirl around, those with green-dotted cups clap their hands three times, and those with blue-dotted cups shout, "Yoo-hoo!" Then have children sit back down, turn over their cups, mix them up, and play again.

Have children form pairs and play a matching game by turning all the cups upside down and then by turning over two cups at a time.

Be sure to send the color cups home along with copies of the Direction Box.

Color Cups

OBJECT: To recognize colors and practice sorting

1. Have your child choose one of the four cups to begin the game.

2. Help your child hunt around the house to find small items the same color of the dot that's inside the cup. Have your child fill the cup with the small items.

3. Repeat the steps, having your child fill each of the cups with appropriately colored items.

CRAFT SUMMARY:
Create colorful arks to hold
lots of animals.

LEARNING GOAL:
To practice sorting and
matching

LESSON CONNECTION:
Use this idea when children
are learning about Noah.

**SPRINKLING OF
SUPPLIES:**
You'll need scissors, construction paper, tape, animal stickers, a large bag of animal
crackers, a large plastic bowl,
and an empty rectangular-
shaped tissue box for each
child. You may also want to
use a large tablecloth during
the game.

PRIOR PREP:
For each child, cut out a simple person shape from the
construction paper. For ease,
trace around a large ginger-
bread man cookie cutter.
Photocopy the Direction Box
from the next page for each
child.

Animal Arks

CREATING THE CRAFT

Craft Time:
10 min.

Explain to the children that they'll be making arks to keep the animals safe during the
flood. Give each child an empty rectangular-shaped tissue
box. Set out animal stickers, and encourage children to use
the stickers to decorate their boxes. Once children have finished, give each child a cutout person shape you made
prior to class. Help children use tape to secure the person
(Noah) into the opening at the top of the tissue box. Each
box should look like a boat with Noah peeking
out the top.

When children have fin-
ished making the animal arks,
play the following learning
game together.

PLAYING THE GAME

Game Time:
10 min.

Spread out a large tablecloth on the floor.
Let children sit in a circle around the tablecloth. Place the animal crackers in the large plastic bowl,
and put the bowl on the floor in the center of the tablecloth. Have children take turns scooping up a handful of
animals to put near their arks. Once everyone has a group
of animals near his or her ark, have children begin sorting
the animals.

Explain that God wanted two of every kind of animal
in the ark. Invite children to help each other make pairs of
animals to go inside their arks. If children end up with single animals, have them hunt for companion animals in
the bowl. Have children play until everyone has made at
least two or three matches; then let children enjoy marching their animals into their arks. As children march the
animals into their arks, have them identify the animals'

names and imitate the sounds they make. Once all the animals are safely inside the arks, you may want to have children enjoy their animal pairs as a snack.

Be sure to send the animal arks home along with copies of the Direction Box.

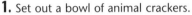

Animal Arks

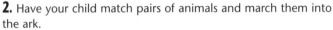

OBJECT: To practice sorting and matching

1. Set out a bowl of animal crackers.

2. Have your child match pairs of animals and march them into the ark.

3. As your child puts each animal inside the ark, have him or her say the animal's name and imitate its sound.

● Read the story of Noah and the flood, and let children act it out.

● Use the arks to sort shapes and colors.

CRAFT SUMMARY:
Reveal a secret letter with crayon rubbings.

LEARNING GOAL:
To develop projection and fine motor skills

LESSON CONNECTION:
Use this idea when children are learning that God is real even though we can't see him.

SPRINKLING OF SUPPLIES:
You'll need small, resealable manila envelopes; thin cardboard; scissors; crayons; and markers.

PRIOR PREP:
Cut the thin cardboard into letters that will fit inside the manila envelopes. Each child will need at least five letters. Photocopy the Direction Box from the next page for each child.

Surprise Letters

CREATING THE CRAFT

Craft Time:
10 min.

Give each child five thin cardboard letters. Have the children use watercolor markers to decorate the letters with doodles and designs. Older preschoolers will enjoy practicing their penmanship by decorating their cardboard letters with written letters and with pictures of things that start with that letter.

When the children have finished making the surprise letters, play the following learning game together.

PLAYING THE GAME

Game Time:
10 min.

For each child, secretly put one of the five letters inside a manila envelope. Hand out crayons. Show the children how to unwrap a crayon, lay it flat on an envelope, and color to make a rubbing of the cardboard letter inside. Have each child rub a crayon on an envelope until he or she can guess what letter is inside. Open the envelopes to see if the children's predictions are correct; then have children think of words that begin with that letter.

To play again, secretly put another letter in each child's envelope, turning the envelope around so the child will make a crayon rubbing on the blank side of the envelope.

Once children understand the concept of the game,

encourage them to guess what the letters are after they've rubbed the crayon over a very small portion of the letter. Talk about the characteristics of the letters; for example, some letters only have straight edges and some letters only have curved edges.

For a more advanced game, secretly put a letter in each child's envelope and have the child predict what the letter will be just by feeling the letter.

You can also play this game with shapes and numbers.

Be sure to send the surprise letters and several blank manila envelopes home along with copies of the Direction Box.

Surprise Letters

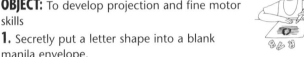

OBJECT: To develop projection and fine motor skills

1. Secretly put a letter shape into a blank manila envelope.

2. Have your child make a crayon rubbing of the letter until he or she can predict what letter it is.

3. Open the envelope and see if your child is right.

4. Help your child think of words that begin with that letter.

CRAFT SUMMARY:
Make flower masks from
paper plates and construction
paper triangles.

LEARNING GOAL:
To exercise the imagination
and large motor skills

LESSON CONNECTION:
Use this idea when children
are learning about God's
care.

SPRINKLING OF SUPPLIES:
You'll need inexpensive paper
plates, several bright colors of
construction paper, glue
sticks, tape, scissors, an
empty watering can, cup-
cakes, frosting, plastic knives,
fruit leather, gumdrops, and
craft sticks.

PRIOR PREP:
For each child, cut out the
center of a paper plate to
form a "frame" that the child
can see through.
Photocopy the Direction Box
from the next page for each
child.

Flowers-of-the-Field Masks

CREATING THE CRAFT

Craft Time:
15 min.

Give each child a paper plate with the center cut out of it. Show children how to tear triangles out of construction paper and use glue sticks to glue the triangles onto their plates to form flower petals. When children's flowers are finished, have each child tape a craft stick to the edge of the plate as a handle.

When children have finished making the flowers-of-the-field masks, play the following learning game together.

PLAYING THE GAME

Game Time:
10 min.

Have the children stand in a circle with their flower masks on the floor in front of them. Have the children pretend to be seeds and curl up into small balls.

Turn the lights out, and say: **This is how a seed might feel in the ground when it's planted.** Turn on the lights, and say: **A seed needs sunshine to help it grow out of the ground.** Using a watering can, pretend to water the flower seeds. Say: **God provides water for the seeds to grow by making it rain.** Tell children to pretend to be seeds growing into plants by stretching until they're standing up straight. Have them hold their flower masks to their faces and wave and dance in the sunshine.

For a fun treat, make flower cupcakes with cupcakes, frosting, plastic knives, fruit leather, and gumdrops. Frost the cupcakes. Give each child one gumdrop, and have children smash their gumdrops with their thumbs to make flat gumdrops. Pay close attention, because unsmashed gumdrops are a choking hazard. Have the children arrange small bits of fruit leather around the edges of the cupcakes to resemble flowers.

Be sure to send home the flowers-of-the-field masks along with copies of the Direction Box.

Extension Idea

● Bring in flowers, and let the children take them apart to see what an interesting creator their God is.

Flowers-of-the-Field Masks

OBJECT: To exercise the imagination and large motor skills

1. Have your child curl up in a tight ball and pretend to be a seed.
2. Pretend to water the seed.
3. Have "the seed" pretend to grow by standing up and stretching.
4. Have your child hold the flower mask to his or her face and dance and wave in the "sunshine."

Whoops-a-Daisy

CREATING THE CRAFT

Craft Time:
10 min.

Set out the colored dot stickers and crayons or markers. Give each child three index cards. Show the children how to make daisies by arranging five dots in a circle and then by putting a dot of a different color in the center. Help the children draw stems and leaves with crayons or markers. You may want to write the word "whoops" at the top of each card. Have each child make three cards. Put the children's names on their cards.

When children have finished making the whoops-a-daisy cards, play the following learning game together.

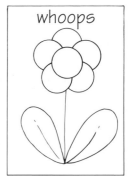

whoops

PLAYING THE GAME

Game Time:
10 min.

Sit in a circle with the children. Have the children each line up their three cards in front of them on the floor. Say: **I'm going to tell you a story. Somewhere in the middle of the story, I'll say something that doesn't make sense. When people make mistakes, sometimes they say, "Whoops-a-daisy." So when I make a mistake in the story, pick up one of your whoops-a-daisy cards and hold it high in the air.**

Tell a simple story about something the children are familiar with. For example, you might tell a story about a child getting ready for bed at night. In the middle of the story, tell something in the wrong order or mention something that isn't likely to happen. For example, during the story about the child getting ready for bed, you might say that she put her pajamas on and then she took off her clothes, or that she swam down the hallway to the bathroom to brush her teeth.

When the children hold up their cards, ask them what mistake you made. Have the children tell you what the mistake was; then have everyone turn one card upside down. Then tell another story.

At the beginning of the game, make the mistakes very obvious. But as the children catch on to the game, make the mistakes harder to catch. Older preschoolers will enjoy telling their own stories.

Be sure to send the whoops-a-daisy cards home along with copies of the Direction Box.

Whoops-a-Daisy

whoops

OBJECT: To practice careful listening

1. Have your child lay out the whoops-a-daisy cards in front of him or her.

2. Tell a story about something you do every day, but make a mistake in the story. For example, tell a story about getting ready for bed, and have the character put on her pajamas before she takes off her clothes, or have her swim down the hallway to the bathroom to brush her teeth.

3. Have your child listen for the mistake. When your child hears a mistake, have him or her hold up a whoops-a-daisy card high in the air.

4. Have your child tell you what the mistake was and turn the card over. Tell another story.

5. When your child has used every card, have him or her tell you the stories.

CRAFT SUMMARY:
Decorate little-lamb game envelopes.

LEARNING GOAL:
To improve memory and recall

LESSON CONNECTION:
Use this idea when children are learning about the little lost sheep.

SPRINKLING OF SUPPLIES:
You'll need a pen; manila envelopes; glue; crayons; cotton balls; and small "treasures" such as rocks, crayons, and sticks.

PRIOR PREP:
For each child, draw an oval shape on a manila envelope. The oval shapes will become the bodies of the sheep. Photocopy the Direction Box from the next page for each child.

Little Lamb, What's Missing?

CREATING THE CRAFT

Craft Time: 15 min.

Set out the glue, cotton balls, and crayons. Give each child a manila envelope. Have the children glue cotton balls inside the ovals to make the bodies of the sheep. Invite the children to draw legs and heads on the lambs. While the children are working, tell them the story of the little lost lamb from Luke 15:1-7.

When children have finished decorating the envelopes, give each child five small treasures to put inside his or her envelope. To avoid a choking danger with young children, make sure none of the treasures are smaller than a fifty-cent piece. For extra fun, have the children collect these items themselves. Choose items such as rocks, crayons, sticks, and small toys. You could also choose small food items.

When children have finished making the little-lamb envelopes, play the following learning game together.

Game Time: 10 min.

Have the children sit on the floor in a circle. Using one little-lamb envelope, begin the game by taking two treasures out of the envelope and showing them to the children. Then cover the items with the envelope, and secretly hide one of the treasures in your lap. Then move the envelope to reveal the remaining treasure. Ask: **Little lamb, what's missing?** Have the children tell you which item is missing. Then play again.

As children catch on to the game, add items until you're playing with all five treasures. Then let the children be the ones to hide the treasure and ask, "What's missing?"

Next, play the game in reverse. Start with one treasure, and then add another. Ask: **Little lamb, what's new?** You can also use the treasures for an adding or subtracting game. Explain that adding means we put the items all together and count them; subtracting means we take away some items from a bigger group of items. Ask: **If I take one away, how many are left?**

Be sure to send the little-lamb envelopes home along with copies of the Direction Box.

Extension Idea

● Have children make lip-smackin' lambies. Put graham cracker pieces on a plate to create a lamb's "body" and "head." Spread white frosting on the pieces. Add miniature chocolate chips for eyes, noses, and mouths. Sprinkle coconut on top for lambs' wool, and use straight pretzels for legs. For extra fun, the children can eat the snacks with a partner. Have them shut their eyes, eat up part of the lamb and ask, "Little lamb, what's missing?"

Little Lamb, What's Missing?

OBJECT: To improve memory and recall

1. Take two of the five treasures out of the envelope. Name the treasures.

2. Hide the treasures by holding the envelope in front of them.

3. Secretly remove one treasure. Move the envelope and ask, "Little lamb, what's missing?" Have your child guess what item is missing.

4. As your child catches on, add more items until you're playing with all five treasures. Then let your child hide the treasures.

CRAFT SUMMARY:
Create floating umbrellas for a shower of blessings.

LEARNING GOAL:
To improve coordination and aim

LESSON CONNECTION:
Use this idea when children are learning about God's good gifts.

SPRINKLING OF SUPPLIES:
You'll need one paper muffin cup for each child, pipe cleaners, markers, a hole punch, and tape.

PRIOR PREP:
Punch a hole in center of each muffin cup.
Photocopy the Direction Box from the next page for each child.

Shower of Blessings

CREATING THE CRAFT

Craft Time: 15 min.

Set out markers, and give each child a muffin cup. Have the children decorate the muffin cups with the markers. Then give each child a pipe cleaner, and show children how to bend it into a hook shape. Have the children hold their muffin cups upside down and then poke the straight end of the pipe cleaners up through the hole from the bottom. Then show children how to bend the top bit of the pipe cleaner at a ninety-degree angle so the pipe cleaner stays attached to the muffin cup. Put a piece of tape over the top of pipe cleaner to keep it attached to the muffin cup. Be sure to write each child's name on his or her "umbrella."

When children have finished making the shower-of-blessings umbrellas, play the following learning game together.

PLAYING THE GAME

Game Time: 10 min.

Have the children stand in a circle and hold their shower-of-blessings umbrellas. Say: **God has given us many good gifts. We call those gifts "blessings." Let's think about the gifts we have from God. When I say "go," toss your umbrella up in the air, and call out a blessing before it hits the ground. Keep tossing up your umbrella and calling out blessings until I say "stop."**

Have children play the game. With young children, you may want them to take turns tossing umbrellas and calling out blessings. With older children, have them call out as many blessings as they can before the umbrellas hit the ground.

For even more fun, have the children draw self-portraits on small paper plates. Have them put the portraits on the floor in front of them and "shower" themselves with the muffin cup umbrellas.

Be sure to send the shower-of-blessings umbrellas home along with copies of the Direction Box.

Extension Idea

● Make extra muffin cup umbrellas, and use them to serve "raindrops of blessings." Make blue finger-gelatin according to the instructions on the box. Scoop out the gelatin with a melon baller, and serve it in the umbrellas.

Rock Patterns

CREATING THE CRAFT

Craft Time: 10 min.

Have the children color their rocks in four different colors so they have two rocks of each color. This craft works equally well with crayons, markers, or paints. If children use crayons, they'll find it easier to color the rocks if the rocks have been warmed outside in the sunshine. Just make sure the rocks don't get hot enough to burn the children's hands.

If you have time, have the children also decorate the lunch bags.

When children have finished making the rock patterns, play the following learning game together.

PLAYING THE GAME

Game Time: 10 min.

Have each child put four rocks of different colors into their bags and set the other four rocks aside. Have children shake the bags gently and then roll the rocks out of the bag. Have the children line up the rocks in the order they came out of the bag. Then have the children call out the color pattern—for example, blue, purple, yellow, and green. Then have the children arrange their other four rocks into the same pattern. Play again and again.

You can also play the pattern game on a grander scale. Have children form pairs. Tape construction paper sheets to the front of each child's shirt, being sure to give each pair of children a different color of paper. Then have the children stand in a circle without standing next to their partners. Walk around the circle, and tap several children on the head. Have these children line up in the middle of the circle. Then have everyone call out the color pattern of the children who are lined up—for example, blue, pink, red, and green. Then have the children's partners line up next to them in the middle of the circle.

Be sure to send the rock patterns home along with copies of the Direction Box.

Rock Patterns

OBJECT: To practice pattern recognition

1. Have your child put four rocks of different colors into the bag.

2. Let your child pour the rocks out.

3. Help your child line up the rocks in the order they came out of the bag and call out the color pattern.

4. Help your child line up the four remaining rocks in the same color pattern.

Extension Idea

● Use this idea when children are learning about stone altars. Have children arrange their pile of rocks into an "altar."

Twirling Umbrellas

CREATING THE CRAFT

Craft Time: 10 min.

Give each child a paper plate. Have each child use only two primary-colored crayons to color the wedges on their paper plates. Show the children what it means to alternate their colors. For example, a child could color the wedges in a "red, yellow, red, yellow" pattern.

Then have the children turn their plates color-side down. Show the children how to press a straw down against the plate to spread out the four sections that were created when you cut the X in the straw. Help children tape down the four "spokes" of the straw to create the handle of the umbrellas.

When children have finished making the twirling umbrellas, play the following learning game together.

TEACHER TIP

If you use bendable straws, cut the X into the end farthest away from the bend. This way, kids can bend the ends of the straws to look like umbrella handles.

PLAYING THE GAME

Game Time: 15 min.

Have the children sit on the floor holding their umbrellas. Have each child identify the colors of his or her umbrella. Have the children hold their umbrellas with the handles between their palms. Say:

Watch what happens to the colors. Have the children rub their palms together so that the umbrellas twirl quickly. The children will see an optical illusion that blends the two primary colors together. Red and yellow will look orange. Red and blue will look purple. And blue and yellow will look green. Have the children tell you what they see when they twirl the umbrellas quickly.

To maximize learning, have the children enjoy mixing colors in other media. Tint white frosting with different colors of food coloring. Have the children experiment by mixing small amounts of the frosting together to create new colors. Spread the frosting on graham crackers, and ask the children if the different colors taste different. Don't be surprised if children think the purple frosting tastes different from the green frosting!

Be sure to send the twirling umbrellas home along with copies of the Direction Box.

Twirling Umbrellas

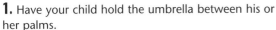

OBJECT: To practice color mixing

1. Have your child hold the umbrella between his or her palms.

2. Ask your child to identify the colors.

3. Let your child twirl the umbrella quickly between his or her palms.

4. Ask your child what happens to the colors when the umbrella twirls.

Permission to photocopy this box from *More Than Mud Pies* granted for local church use.
Copyright © Group Publishing, Inc., P.O. Box 481, Loveland, CO 80539.

Hungry Boxes

CREATING THE CRAFT

Craft Time:
15 min.

Give each child a large sheet of paper, a piece of cardboard, and a tissue box. Show the children how to tape the folded edge of a cardboard piece to a tissue box as shown in the illustration below. Then have children tape or glue the construction paper sheet over the cardboard piece and the tissue box. Have children trim the cardboard to match the size of the paper.

Poke a hole through the opening of the tissue box; then have children trim the paper away from the hole.

Have the children draw eyes and noses on their cardboard. Show children how the tissue-box hole forms a "mouth."

Set the hungry boxes aside while the glue dries. Help the children gather at least twenty-five magazine pictures in various categories such as food, toys, people, buildings, or vehicles.

When children have finished making the hungry boxes and gathering the pictures, play the following learning game together.

PLAYING THE GAME

Game Time:
10 min.

Have each child sit with his or her box and pile of pictures. Have the children mix up their pictures.

Then say: **These mouths are very hungry, but they only like to eat certain things. Right now, the mouths would like to eat some food. Who has some food for their mouth to eat?**

Have the children put pictures of food items inside the mouths of their hungry boxes. When all the food pictures have been "fed" to the boxes, have the children take those pictures out of the boxes; then choose another category, such as people. Play until all the children's picture categories have been used in the game.

You can also use the hungry boxes to teach color and shape sorting, and to increase children's powers of observation. Have the children search their pictures for certain colors or for certain shapes.

Be sure to send the hungry boxes home along with copies of the Direction Box.

Hungry Boxes

OBJECT: To practice sorting by category

1. Have your child mix up the pictures.
2. Choose a category such as food, people, or vehicles.
3. Have your child feed pictures of things in that category to the box.
4. Choose another category.
5. Play until all the pictures have been "fed" to the box.

Extension Idea

● Feed the "hungry mouths" in your class a "category" snack. Make a trail mix of various shapes, colors, and sizes of treats. Give each child a handful on a paper towel. Call out a category, such as squares, and have the children search through their trail mix for square tidbits to eat.

Creation Bingo

CREATING THE CRAFT

Craft Time:
15 min.

Give each child a "Creation Bingo" handout (p. 84), and help him or her glue the game grid to a piece of cardboard. Let children color and decorate their game boards and then cover the game boards with clear Con-Tact paper. Have the children press down on the Con-Tact paper to get rid of any air bubbles. While the children are working, talk about God's Creation.

When children have finished making the creation bingo game boards, play the following learning game together.

PLAYING THE GAME

Game Time:
15 min.

Make sure each child has a game board and a crayon. Take children for a walk, and have them search for the items on their creation bingo game board. As children spot each item, have them cross it off with the crayons. When someone has found and marked off all the pictures, have him or her say, "God made the world!" Wipe marks off with damp paper towels, and play again.

For even more fun, spread ten natural items on a table. Have the children take a good look at all the items. Cover the objects with a towel, take one of the items away, and conceal it completely in your hand. Lift off the towel, and have the children try to figure out which item is missing. Return the hidden object to the table. Let the child who figured out what was missing have a turn hiding an item.

Another idea is to use several ropes to mark off a ten-foot square outside on a grass or yard area. Have children use magnifying lenses and pretend to be detectives or scientists. Your children will discover an amazing array of created things.

Be sure to send the creation bingo game boards home along with copies of the Direction Box.

Creation Bingo

OBJECT: To develop observation and identification skills

1. Take your child for a walk to search for the items on the creation bingo game board.

2. Have your child use a crayon to mark each item he or she discovers.

3. When your child has marked each picture, have him or her say, "God created the world!" Then erase the marks with a damp paper towel, and play again.

Creation Bingo

SECTION FOUR:

Number Skills

CRAFT SUMMARY:

Make and decorate blocks from paper lunch bags.

LEARNING GOAL:

To improve number concepts and balancing skills

LESSON CONNECTION:

Use this activity when your class is learning about Nehemiah.

SPRINKLING OF SUPPLIES:

You'll need plain paper lunch sacks, tissue paper or a box of facial tissues, two or three sponges, two or three pie pans, paper towels, scissors, water, tempera paint, and cleanup supplies. You may want to use paint smocks or old shirts.

PRIOR PREP:

Cut the sponges into two- or three-inch shapes such as a circle, a square, a rectangle, and a triangle. Dampen the sponges, and squeeze out any excess water.

Photocopy the Direction Box from the next page for each child.

Bagging and Blocking

CREATING THE CRAFT

Craft Time: 20 min.

Give each child two paper lunch bags and a pile of tissue paper. Show the children how to crumple the tissue paper and use the crumpled tissue paper to fill one of the bags. Help each child slide the open end of the filled bags into the empty bag to form a soft, light-weight block. Have each child make five blocks.

TEACHER TIP

Making a "stamp pad" makes this activity less messy. Set a stack of paper towels in a pie pan, and saturate them with thin tempera paint. Have the children press the sponges onto the paper towels to lightly coat the sponges with paint. With this method, the sponges won't be dripping with paint, and the children are less likely to have projects that drip and run with too much paint.

Have the children decorate the sides of their blocks. Set out tempera paint in pie pans and the dampened shape sponges. Young children know how to brush or rub paint on paper, but they may not know how to sponge-paint. Show the children how to lightly dip the sponges in the paint and gently press the sponges onto the blocks. Then show children how to carefully lift the sponges to create "prints" with crisp edges.

Young children may be tempted to pound the sponges on the blocks. Tell the children to be gentle with the sponge painting. If they aren't gentle, they'll flatten their bricks, the painted shapes will be distorted, or the paint might splatter.

When the children have finished painting, set the bags aside to dry. When the bags are dry, play the following learning game.

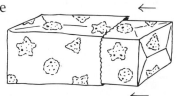

Game Time:
10 min.

Say: **We can work together as the people who helped Nehemiah did. Let's build a wall together.**

Ask each child to hold one of his or her blocks. One child will place the first block into the wall and say, "One block." Another child will place the next block either next to the first block or on top of it and say, "Two blocks." Continue building until all the children have placed their blocks into the wall and have counted the number of their blocks. Praise the children for working together, and review the story of Nehemiah.

Be sure to send the bag blocks home along with copies of the Direction Box.

Bagging and Blocking

OBJECT: To improve number concepts and balancing skills

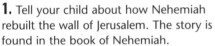
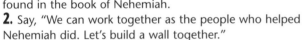

1. Tell your child about how Nehemiah rebuilt the wall of Jerusalem. The story is found in the book of Nehemiah.

2. Say, "We can work together as the people who helped Nehemiah did. Let's build a wall together."

3. Have your child put the first block in position and say, "One block."

4. Then place the next block on top of the first block and say, "Two blocks." Have your child put the third block on top and say, "Three blocks."

5. See how many ways you can put the blocks together to make different kinds of walls. You might stack them end-on-end to make a tall vertical tower or wall. Or you might draw a picture of Jerusalem and make a triangular wall around it with the blocks.

Extension Ideas

● Use this idea when children are learning about David's youth. Build a sheepfold with the blocks, and encourage the children to be the "sheep" inside.

● Adapt this idea to use when your lesson is about Joshua and the walls of Jericho. Build the wall just as it is described in the game. Then knock it down.

CRAFT SUMMARY:
Create cotton ball sheep and a place for them to sleep.

LEARNING GOAL:
To practice counting

LESSON CONNECTION:
Use this idea when children are learning that Jesus is the good shepherd.

SPRINKLING OF SUPPLIES:
You'll need scissors, a paper plate, toothpicks or cotton swabs, cotton balls, black construction paper, paper cups, a hole punch, glue sticks, and tacky craft glue.

PRIOR PREP:
Cut half-inch-by-two-inch strips of construction paper. You'll need at least four strips for each child. Using the hole punch, make twenty black construction paper dots for each child. Have extra construction paper strips and dots on hand.
Photocopy the Direction Box from the next page for each child.

CREATING THE CRAFT

Craft Time: 15 min.

Set out the glue sticks and the construction paper strips and dots. Give each child a paper cup. Show the children how to glue strips of construction paper in vertical stripes on a cup. Explain that children are putting a "fence" around the cups to make a sheepfold, a safe place for sheep to live.

While the children are working, say: **The Bible says that Jesus is like a shepherd. Shepherds take care of sheep. They make sure the sheep have clean water to drink and plenty of grass to eat. The Bible says that we are like the sheep. Jesus takes care of us as a shepherd takes care of sheep.**

TEACHER TIP
Before older preschoolers glue the "fences" on their cups, they'll enjoy using watercolor markers to draw grass for the sheep to eat and water for the sheep to drink.

After children have decorated their cups, give each child ten cotton balls. Help the children use a small amount of tacky craft glue to place two small paper eyes on each of their cotton balls. Put a small puddle of glue on a paper plate, and provide flat toothpicks or cotton swabs for children to use to apply glue to the paper pieces.

When children have finished making the sheep and their sheepfolds, play the following learning game together.

Baa! Baa! Baa!

PLAYING THE GAME

Game Time: 10 min.

Have the children sit on the floor with their sheep in front of them. Instruct children to hold their paper cups in their hands and say the following rhyme with you:

Jesus wants to count his sheep
And tuck them in to go to sleep.
> (Count to ten, and direct the children to put one sheep in the sheepfold cup for each number counted. Then continue with the end of the rhyme.)

Now wake them up and start again!

Once children put all the sheep in their cups, let children spill out the sheep to play again.

Be sure to send the sheep and sheepfolds home along with copies of the Direction Box.

Extension Ideas

● For older children, increase the number of cotton ball sheep to count.

● Help children take the sheep out one at a time while they count backward.

Counting Sheep

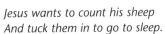

OBJECT: To practice counting

1. Help your child repeat the following rhyme while putting sheep in the paper cup one at a time.

Jesus wants to count his sheep
And tuck them in to go to sleep.
> (Count to ten, and direct your child to put one sheep in the sheepfold cup for each number counted. Then continue with the end of the rhyme.)

Now wake them up and start again!

2. Let your child spill the sheep back out and start the game again.

CRAFT SUMMARY:
Make paper plate portraits with countable hairs.

LEARNING GOAL:
To practice counting and following directions

LESSON CONNECTION:
Use this idea when children are learning about God's care as expressed in Matthew 10:30—"And even the very hairs of your head are all numbered."

SPRINKLING OF SUPPLIES:
You'll need scissors, paper plates, markers, construction paper, tape, glue, toothpicks or cotton swabs, and colorful yarn.

PRIOR PREP:
Cut out shapes for eyes, noses, and mouths from the construction paper. You'll also need to cut yarn into five-inch lengths. You'll need ten pieces of yarn for each child. Photocopy the Direction Box from the next page for each child.

Hairs on My Head

CREATING THE CRAFT

Craft Time: 10 min.

Set out paper plates, markers, and the construction paper shapes. Put a small puddle of glue on a paper plate, and provide flat toothpicks or cotton swabs for children to use to apply glue to paper pieces.

Have the children use the shapes and markers to make paper plate portraits of themselves by making the paper plates look as much like themselves as possible. Talk about what features children should include in the portraits—for example, eyes; noses; mouths; and other characteristics such as freckles, eyebrows, and ears.

Give each child ten pieces of yarn. Help children tape the yarn onto their paper plates to make hair.

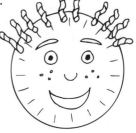

When children have finished making the paper plate portraits and the portraits have dried, play the following learning game together.

PLAYING THE GAME

Game Time: 10 min.

Have children line up in a single file line. Explain that each child will take a turn giving directions to the other children and then counting the hairs on the top of his or her paper plate portrait. For example, the first child in line might say, "While I count, you can hop" or "While I count, you can twirl" and then begin counting the hairs. Older preschoolers will have fun thinking up actions. Younger preschoolers may need your help. Have children follow the direction for each hair the counter counts.

Begin the game with the first person in line. After that child has chosen an action and has counted all the hairs on his or her plate, have him or her go to the back of the line. Then have the next person in line choose an action for the others to do while counting the hairs on his or her plate.

Continue playing until each child has had a turn counting and giving the group an action.

Be sure to send the paper plate portraits home along with copies of the Direction Box.

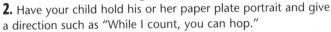

Hairs on My Head

OBJECT: To practice counting and following directions

1. Read Matthew 10:30 together.

2. Have your child hold his or her paper plate portrait and give a direction such as "While I count, you can hop."

3. While your child counts the "hairs" on his or her paper plate portrait, hop once each time your child counts.

4. Take the paper plate, and give your child a direction such as "While I count, you can pat your head." Then count the hairs while your child pats his or her head each time you count.

Extension Ideas

● Use the process of taping to teach simple addition. Help children count before adding another piece of yarn and then discover that they know how to add one to any number.

● Use this activity when your children are learning about Samson.

Wisdom Wallets

CREATING THE CRAFT

Craft Time: 20 min.

Show the children the dollar bills you brought. Say: **People use money to buy things they need from the store. Many people keep their money in wallets or billfolds. Let's make wallets.**

Give each child an envelope; then set out crayons and markers for the children to decorate their envelope "wallets." Help the children write their names on their wallets. Encourage children to create designs and patterns around the edges of the wallets.

Give each child a long piece of green crepe paper to tear up into ten dollar-bills. The children can also use markers to decorate the crepe paper to look like dollar bills. Show them what a dollar bill looks like, and talk about the pictures and words that appear on money. While the children are working, ask them what they'd like to buy with their money. Have the children put their play money into their wallets.

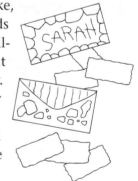

When children have finished making the wisdom wallets, play the following learning game together.

PLAYING THE GAME

Game Time: 10 min.

Take the children to the area where you've set up the pretend store. Give each child a napkin to hold their "purchases." Have the children "buy" items from the store. Each "dollar bill" buys one cracker or fruit chunk. Ask each child, "What would you like to buy?" and "How many would you like to buy?" If children say they'd like to buy three Goldfish crackers, have them count out three dollar bills and lay them out in a row. Then count out three Goldfish crackers, and lay them out in a row. Older children might like to take turns being the shop-keeper. While the children are enjoying their treats, review the Bible story.

When the children have spent all their money and have enjoyed their purchases, hand their money back to them and play again.

Be sure to send the wisdom wallets home along with copies of the Direction Box.

Extension Ideas

● Take a pretend offering. Then have the children decide how to spend the money to buy things to help others.

● Hide some of the money, and have the children hunt for it. This game works well when you're teaching the lesson of the lost coin.

Wisdom Wallets

OBJECT: To learn about counting and number correspondence

1. Set up a store with small, snack-item merchandise such as crackers.

2. Have your child decide what and how many he or she would like to buy. For example, your child might want to buy two fruit chunks and three round crackers.

3. Have your child count out two "dollar bills" for the fruit chunks and three for the crackers.

4. Count out two fruit chunks and three crackers, and lay them beside the dollar bills.

5. When your child has spent all the money and eaten all the treats, give the money back and play again.

Sailing Ships

CREATING THE CRAFT

Craft Time:
15 min.

Have the children use stickers to decorate their banana-split boats. Cut an X in the bottom of the straws so when the four edges are spread out on the bottom of the boats, they can be taped down to hold the "mast" in place. Have the children thread a five-by-five-inch construction paper "sail" onto each mast. Help children tape the masts in the bottoms of the boats.

Tie a large knot on the end of a piece of string, and pull the string through the hole in the front of the boats to make pull strings. Use a permanent marker to write children's names on their boats.

When children have finished making the sailing ships, play the following learning game together.

PLAYING THE GAME

Game Time:
10 min.

Have each child put four boats aside. Have the children line up on one side of the room, which is the "shore." Then have them pull their boats around the room while you recite the following rhyme. When you get to the line, "One little ship hurried back to shore," tap a child on the head, and have him or her leave the game, sit on the floor, and recite the rhyme with you. Continue reciting the rhyme until all the children are sitting.

> (Name the number of students) *little boats went on a trip.*
> *Along came a storm and blew the ships.* (Make a wind sound.)
> *One little ship hurried back to shore,*

While (number of remaining children and boats) *little boats stayed out for more.* (Have the children return to the "shore.")

At the end of the game, say:

Now the sea is smooth as glass,
And we can sail our ships so fast.
Jesus calmed the stormy sea.
He will keep us safe—you'll see.

Be sure to send the sailing ships home along with copies of the Direction Box.

Extension Idea

● While you're making the boats, direct children to draw a picture of a person, color it, and cut it out. Depending on which Bible story you're using, the children can put the character from the story into their boats for the learning game.

Sailing Ships

OBJECT: To practice subtracting and sequencing

1. Choose an area of the room to be the "shore" and an area to be the "water." Have your child pull all five boats out into the sea.

2. Say the following rhyme while your child leads his or her boats, one by one, to the shore. Continue saying the rhyme, changing the numbers, until all the boats are back at shore.

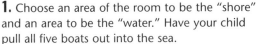
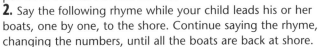

> *Five little boats went on a trip.*
> *Along came a storm and blew the ships.* (Make a wind sound.)
> *One little ship hurried back to shore,*
> *While four little boats stayed out for more.*

3. Say the following rhyme after your child has retrieved all the boats and brought them back to shore.

> *Now the sea is smooth as glass,*
> *And we can sail our ships so fast.*
> *Jesus calmed the stormy sea.*
> *He will keep us safe—you'll see.*

What's a Dozen?

CREATING THE CRAFT

Craft Time: 15 min.

Give each child an egg carton. Instruct children to use glue, paper or ribbon scraps, and markers to decorate the outsides of their counting boxes. Give each child a set of one to twelve stickers, and have children stick the stickers to the bottoms of their egg cartons in the order illustrated below.

When children have finished making the "what's a dozen?" counting boxes, play the following learning game together.

PLAYING THE GAME

Game Time: 10 min.

Explain that some things, such as fingers and toes, come in tens but other things, such as eggs and doughnuts, come in dozens. Show the children a counting box, and explain that a dozen is twelve of something. Tell the children that Jesus had twelve disciples.

Then say: **Let's pretend we have a dozen cats. Let's count a dozen cats.** Have the children point to the numbers in their boxes as they count, "One cat, two cats, three cats..." and on up to twelve cats.

Have each child pick out something else to count a dozen of. Children might pick items such as dogs, cupcakes, eggs, doughnuts, or disciples. Whatever they pick, count twelve of them, and have the children point to each number in the box as they say the number.

Hand each child a bag of cereal. Call out a number

between one and twelve, and have the children find that number in their boxes. Have the children count out that number of cereal pieces and put them in the correct spot in the box. Continue calling out numbers until the children have filled up all of the holes in their boxes; then have children return the cereal pieces to the resealable plastic bags. If you have time, let the children eat the cereal as a snack.

Be sure to send the "what's a dozen?" counting boxes home along with copies of the Direction Box.

What's a Dozen?

OBJECT: To understand number concepts and develop fine motor skills

1. Have your child pick out an object to count twelve of. For example, if your child chooses cats, help him or her count, "One cat, two cats, three cats..." and so on up to twelve. Point to the correct number in the counting box as you count.

2. Call out a number between one and twelve. Have your child find the right number in the counting box and then count out that many cereal pieces. Put the cereal pieces in the corresponding hole in the box.

3. Continue until your child has filled all the box's holes. (You'll need about eighty pieces of cereal.)

Sidebar

CRAFT SUMMARY:
Make colorful measuring cups.

LEARNING GOAL:
To develop counting and measuring skills

LESSON CONNECTION:
Use this idea when children are learning about God's blessings.

SPRINKLING OF SUPPLIES:
You'll need disposable cups; construction paper, fancy paper, or ribbon scraps; a pen; glue; stickers; a big bowl; and several snack items such as crackers, large marshmallows, or chocolate kisses.

PRIOR PREP:
Photocopy the Direction Box from the next page for each child.

CREATING THE CRAFT

Craft Time: 10 min.

Give each child a cup. Have the children decorate the cups by gluing paper scraps to them or by sticking stickers on them. Write each child's name on the bottom of his or her cup.

When children have finished making the overflowing cups, play the following learning game together.

PLAYING THE GAME

Game Time: 10 min.

Read Psalm 23:5 from an easy-to-understand version of the Bible. Say: **God gives us so many good gifts, or blessings, that we sometimes say that our cups run over. That means that God's love and the blessings he gives are so good and so many that our hearts cannot hold them. Let's play a game with our overflowing cups to remind us of all the good things God gives us.**

Have the children fill up their cups with one of the snack items until the cups overflow. Then have the children count how many of a certain snack item it takes to completely fill the cup. Have the children say, "My cup runs over with (number of snack item)."

Have the children compare results. For example, it might take three marshmallows or twelve kisses or twenty round crackers to fill the cup.

Then ask children to name a blessing for each of the items they've put in their cup.

Use the overflowing cups to enjoy a snack. Have each child put a cupful of a different small snack item—such as chocolate chips, Reese's Pieces, and cereal—into a big bowl. Mix the treats together, and have each child scoop out a cupful of treats to enjoy.

Be sure to send the overflowing cups home along with copies of the Direction Box.

Overflowing Cups

OBJECT: To develop counting and measuring skills

1. Read Psalm 23:5, and talk about what it means for your cup to run over with God's blessings.

2. Have your child fill the cup with various objects and count how many it takes to completely fill the cup. For example, it may take three large marshmallows or twelve chocolate kisses or twenty round crackers to fill a cup.

3. Have your child repeat this sentence and fill in the blank: "My cup runs over with (number of objects)."

4. Have your child name a blessing for each of the items he or she placed in the cup.

Extension Idea

● Use this activity with water. Set out undecorated cups, measuring cups, and a basin of water. Have the children discover how many one-fourth-cup measures or one-half-cup measures fill one disposable cup.

CRAFT SUMMARY:
Create a matching-number game.

LEARNING GOAL:
To understand number concepts

LESSON CONNECTION:
Use this idea when your children are learning about Creation.

SPRINKLING OF SUPPLIES:
You'll need colorful permanent markers; sheets of clear, nonadhesive vinyl from a fabric store; plain scrap paper; paper; pen; scissors; and envelopes.

PRIOR PREP:
Write the numbers one through five (or one through ten depending on the abilities of the children) on a sheet of paper. Then photocopy the sheet for each child. Cut the vinyl into two-inch squares. Photocopy the Direction Box from the next page for each child.

Stuck on Numbers

CREATING THE CRAFT

Craft Time:
10 min.

Give each child a photocopy of the numbers, a permanent marker, and several vinyl squares. Provide several different colors of permanent markers, and caution the children to be careful with the markers. You may want to use paint smocks or towels to cover children's torsos.

Have each child put a vinyl square on top of a number on the photocopied sheet and then trace the number. Then on another vinyl square, have the child draw the same number of dots. Let children make as many pairs of numbers and dots as they want. For young preschoolers, the numbers one through five will be enough; older preschoolers can use numbers one through ten.

When children have finished making the number stickers, play the following learning game together.

PLAYING THE GAME

Game Time:
5 min.

Go with children to a window or a mirrored surface, and have them stick their vinyl number pieces on the smooth surface in a mixed-up fashion. Then have children pair up the number and dot pieces and restick them in pairs. When the children have matched a pair of vinyl squares, have them name things that God has created in a category such as colors, animals, or plants.

For a fun variation, have the children try sticking the numbers, and then the dots, in numerical order. Challenge older preschoolers with addition and subtraction questions.

When the children are finished playing, give them envelopes and scrap paper to help store the pieces. Have children put the scrap paper between the vinyl pieces because the ink from one vinyl piece could stick to other vinyl pieces.

Be sure to send the number stickers home along with copies of the Direction Box.

Extension Ideas

● Have the children pair up and play with the number pieces together.

● Have children write letters on the vinyl squares to spell their names or messages such as "I love you" for people to read in a window. This is a great gift idea and is easy to send in the mail.

● Cut the vinyl into rectangles, and have the children make domino window stickers. Draw shapes, colors, or numbers on the vinyl as the domino game.

Serving Supper

CREATING THE CRAFT

Craft Time: 15 min.

Give each child a large piece of construction paper and a paper plate. Show children how to trace around a paper plate in the middle of the construction paper "place mat."

Pass out the cups, and show the children where to trace a cup on a place mat. Then have the children trace, one by one, the napkins, the forks, the knives, and the spoons. Let the children personalize their place mats as they please. Also help children write on each space of their place mats the order in which to set the table. Put a "1" on the plates, a "2" on the cups, a "3" on the napkin, a "4" on the fork, a "5" on the knife, and a "6" on the spoon. While the children are working, tell them the story of Lydia, who offered hospitality to Paul.

You may want to cover the place mats with clear Con-Tact paper. This is especially good for designs done with watercolor markers so the colors don't run when the place mat gets wet.

Hand out resealable plastic bags, and have the children put their plates, cups, napkins, and utensils in the bags.

When children have finished making the place mats, play the following learning game together.

PLAYING THE GAME

Game Time: 5 min.

Let children pretend that they're having a special guest over for dinner and so they want to set the table just right. Encourage children to talk about the important people who've come to their houses for dinner.

Have the children use their place mats to guide them as they set a place for their guest with the tableware. Have children set the table in the order their numbered place mats indicate. Then have children turn their place mats over and see if they can set the place again without the help of the outline.

End by serving a scrumptious snack and eating it with your best company manners.

Be sure to send the place mats and items home along with copies of the Direction Box.

Extension Ideas

● Let children color a dazzling array of delicious foods or glue food pictures from magazines to their paper plates.

● Have each child decorate several place mats with markers. Then laminate the place mats. Have the children take home the place mats to use on their dinner tables.

CRAFT SUMMARY:
Make rings for a fun rhyming game about Rebekah.

LEARNING GOAL:
To develop counting and fine motor skills

LESSON CONNECTION:
Use this idea when children are learning about Isaac meeting Rebekah.

SPRINKLING OF SUPPLIES:
You'll need large marshmallows, colored sugar, paper bowls, and water in a spray bottle. You'll also want to have wet rags to wipe sticky hands.

PRIOR PREP:
Photocopy the Direction Box from the next page for each child.

Rebekah's Rhyme

CREATING THE CRAFT

Craft Time: 10 min.

Say: **Abraham's servant gave jewelry to Rebekah when he found her at the well** (Genesis 24:22). **Let's make some jewelry to remind us of the story.** Give each child five large marshmallows, and explain that they'll get to eat them later. Have the children tear a small hole in the marshmallows so they fit on children's fingers like rings. Then have the children lightly mist the marshmallows with the water and roll the "rings" in the bowls of colored sugar. This activity isn't as messy as it sounds, but you will want to have cleaning supplies handy. Have the children put the rings on one hand.

When children have finished making the rings, act out the following action rhyme together.

PLAYING THE GAME

Game Time: 5 min.

Say: **When it was time for Isaac to get married, a servant gave jewelry to Rebekah, the woman Isaac was supposed to marry. Let's pretend we're Rebekah and our marshmallow rings are the jewels from the servant.** Show the children how to hold up their bejeweled hands and act out this rhyme:

One was the man who came for me. (Hold up one finger.)
Two were the camels—so very thirsty. (Hold up two fingers.)

Three were the rings and bracelets he gave. (Hold up three fingers.)

Four were my family—oh, so brave. (Hold up four fingers)

With my hand I waved "good-bye!" (Use all five fingers to wave)

To be dear Isaac's wife—oh my!

Let children eat their marshmallow rings, and be sure to send home copies of the Direction Box.

Extension Ideas

● Make rings with Gummi Savers and skinny licorice. Say the same rhyme.

● Have your children stretch and pull the marshmallows to make "taffy." Talk about the patience Isaac had when he was waiting to meet Rebekah.

CRAFT SUMMARY:
Make a tree-shaped counting game from egg cartons.

LEARNING GOAL:
To improve counting and number recognition

LESSON CONNECTION:
Use this idea at Christmas-time.

SPRINKLING OF SUPPLIES:
You'll need scissors, glue, poster board, dot stickers, a pen, scrap paper, and markers. You'll also need egg cartons—each child will need fifteen egg cups. You may also want paint and paintbrushes.

PRIOR PREP:
Cut the tops off the egg cartons. Each child will need a single egg-carton cup and a strip each of two cups, three cups, four cups, and five cups. Each child will also need one-fourth of a piece of poster board.
Photocopy the Direction Box from the next page for each child.

Counting Trees

CREATING THE CRAFT

Craft Time: 15 min.

Set out the egg cups, the poster board pieces, and the glue. Show the children how to arrange the egg cups into a pine-tree shape and then glue the bottoms of the cups onto a poster board piece. Have the children use markers to draw stems and decorate the poster board. Write the numbers one through fifteen on a set of dot stickers for each child. Have the children put the dots in order inside the cups.

If you have extra time, you may want to have the children paint the egg cartons before they put the stickers inside.

Set the counting trees aside to dry. When they're dry, play the following learning game together.

PLAYING THE GAME

Game Time: 10 min.

Have the children put their counting trees in front of them on the table or floor. Have children drop small paper wads and see which cups they land in. Have the children identify the numbers and then count from one to that number.

Older children will enjoy practicing counting backward from the number back down to one. Show children how to use the counting tree to help them know what number comes next when counting backward.

You can also use the counting trees for a "more than–less than" game. Call out a number between one and fifteen, and put a marker in the egg cup that corresponds to that number. Have the children drop their paper wad into another cup. Have children use the counting tree to tell if the number is more than or less than the number you called.

Be sure to send the counting trees home along with copies of the Direction Box.

Extension Idea

● Use the counting trees to count the number of days to a special event such as Christmas.

CRAFT SUMMARY:
Make spiders with countable legs.

LEARNING GOAL:
To practice addition and subtraction

LESSON CONNECTION:
Use this activity when children are learning about God's Creation.

SPRINKLING OF SUPPLIES:
You'll need scissors, plastic foam balls, markers, pipe cleaners, glue, cotton candy, plates, pretzel sticks, Double-stuff Oreos, and wiggly eyes.

PRIOR PREP:
Cut the pipe cleaners in half. Each child will need eight halves.
Photocopy the Direction Box from the next page for each child.

Spider Legs

CREATING THE CRAFT

Craft Time:
10 min.

Give each child a plastic foam ball. Set out the markers, and have the children color the foam balls. Give each child two wiggly eyes, and have children glue the eyes to the foam ball.

Then give each child eight pipe cleaner halves, and have the children stick four pipe cleaner legs on each side of the ball to make a spider. Bend the bottoms of the pipe cleaners to form legs.

When children have finished the spiders, play the following learning game together.

PLAYING THE GAME

Game Time:
10 min.

Have each child hold a spider. Say: **God has created a wonderful world full of different kinds of creatures. Some of God's creations have four legs. Can you think of a creature with four legs? Some of God's creatures have two legs. Can you think of a creature with two legs? Some of God's creatures don't have any legs at all. Can you think of a creature without legs? Most bugs have lots of legs. Spiders are bugs. Let's see how many legs spiders have.** Count the legs together. Then say: **Let's take one of the legs out—we'll subtract one leg. How many legs will we have left?** Help the children discover that the answer is "seven." Continue until spiders don't have any more legs. Then reverse the process, adding the legs back, one by one, until there are eight legs attached to each spider.

For even more fun, make a spider-web treat. Have the children pull apart cotton candy so it looks like a spider web. Put the cotton candy on a plate. Cotton candy is often available in movie rental stores. Stick eight short, thin pretzel sticks into the cream of a Doublestuff Oreo, and place the spider on the web. You can also add smashed gumdrop "flies" that have become stuck in the web. Yum!

Be sure to send the spiders home along with copies of the Direction Box.

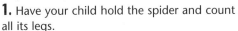
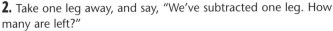
Extension Idea

● Use the spiders to act out the song "Eency Weency Spider."

Group Publishing, Inc.
Attention: Books & Curriculum
P.O. Box 481
Loveland, CO 80539
Fax: (970) 669-1994

Evaluation for *More Than Mud Pies*

Please help Group Publishing, Inc., continue to provide innovative and useful resources for ministry. Please take a moment to fill out this evaluation and mail or fax it to us. Thanks!

● ● ●

1. As a whole, this book has been (circle one)

not very helpful   very helpful

1   2   3   4   5   6   7   8   9   10

2. The best things about this book:

3. Ways this book could be improved:

4. Things I will change because of this book:

5. Other books I'd like to see Group publish in the future:

6. Would you be interested in field-testing future Group products and giving us your feedback? If so, please fill in the information below:

Name _____

Street Address _____

City _____ State _____ Zip _____

Phone Number _____ Date _____

Practical Resources for Your Ministry to Children

Forget-Me-Not Bible Story Activities
Christine Yount

Here's the perfect activity for your elementary-age class—week after week!

Now finding the perfect activity to keep every class right on target is easy—with **Forget-Me-Not Bible Story Activities!**

Each **Forget-Me-Not** lesson includes...
- 7 brand-new activity ideas,
- an "Extra! Extra!" box with fun bonus ideas, and...
- a completely new way to tell the Bible story!

Plus, activities work with any curriculum—and reach *every* kind of learner in your class: verbal, visual, interpersonal, physical, musical, logical, *and* reflective kids!

ISBN 1-55945-633-7

Creative Can-Do Crafts
Lois Keffer

More than 75 all-new craft projects delight even all-thumbs kids—and mostly-thumbs teachers!

Even "noncrafty" teachers love this book!

From simple paper crafts...to zany tie-dye...to edible dirt soufflé, here are enough crafts to keep an elementary class busy for months...and it's easy for teachers.

These crafts are fun to create...fun to carry home...and fun to show to friends! Plus, they encourage your kids' self-confidence and build their Christian faith. Most crafts include Scripture references and Faith Boosters that tie crafts to favorite Bible stories you want your kids to know!

ISBN 1-55945-682-5

Hooray! Let's Pray!
Your children will *want* to pray every day!

You want your kids to pray...and now there's a kid-friendly way to make it happen!

Hooray! Let's Pray! is packed with activities that make prayer part of daily life. Your kids will discover how to pray with others...pray alone...and how to make prayer more than a fold-your-hands-and-bow-your-head time of waiting while someone else talks to God.

These are best-ever ideas from front-line children's workers—specially selected to encourage children from preschool through 5th grade to pray in age-appropriate ways.

BONUS: You'll get practical help explaining why it makes sense for kids to talk to an invisible God!

ISBN 0-7644-2028-3

The Discipline Guide for Children's Ministry
Jody Capehart, Gordon West & Becki West

It's been the hardest thing about teaching...until now.

With this book you'll understand and implement classroom-management techniques that *work*—and that make teaching fun again!

From a thorough explanation of age-appropriate concerns...to proven strategies for heading off discipline problems *before* they occur...here's a practical book you'll turn to again and again.

For appropriate, kid-tested, educationally sound solutions for discipline dilemmas, rely on **The Discipline Guide for Children's Ministry**!

ISBN 1-55945-686-8

Order today from your local Christian bookstore, or write: Group Publishing, P.O. Box 485, Loveland, CO 80539

More Practical Resources for Your Ministry to Children

Ready-to-Do Children's Message Kit
24 memorable children's messages—in one convenient box!

It's all here in one colorful package—everything you need to get kids listening...learning...and wanting to come back for more! There are fun gizmos plus step-by-step directions in an easy-to-use book packed with 24 children's messages. You'll deliver unforgettable, active-learning messages. And you'll appreciate how all the preparation is already done for you! Plus, there's nothing else to buy! There's no need to tack together ideas from a half-dozen expensive resources. Instead, just pull out your **Ready-to-Do Children's Message Kit!**

ISBN 0-7644-2029-1

Ready-to-Do Children's Messages (book only)

ISBN 0-7644-2047-X

Mix & Match Ideas for Preschool Ministry
Leading a class of preschoolers just got easier!

Here are the best-ever preschool ideas from Children's Ministry Magazine!

Tell every preschool teacher you know to mix these ideas...match these ideas...as long as they don't miss these best-ever, fun ideas!

You'll get practical, helpful chapters packed full of Bible Lessons and Story Stretchers, Super Games, Songs and Finger Plays, Best-Ever Crafts, Special Seasons, and Terrific Teacher Tips.

Every idea has been field-tested by preschool leaders across the country, and comes with the Children's Ministry Magazine seal of approval!

ISBN 0-7644-2021-6

Age-Right Play
Susan L. Lingo

For children, play is serious business.

Playing is how young children explore their world...sort out what's safe from what's scary...and build a lifetime of self-confidence and creativity.

And now you'll have the perfect games to help your little ones master the skills they need! Plus, you'll have more fun with your children when you have age-appropriate games ready to play!

ISBN 0-7644-2014-3

Friend-Makers & Crowdbreakers
Help your children's ministry grow!

Helping children feel at home in Sunday school is more than just a good idea—it often determines if visiting families return!

Now it's easy to help children quickly feel comfortable in your Sunday school with these friend-makers and crowdbreakers.

Your teachers will help children...
● meet each other for the first time,
● get to know each other, and
● become real friends!

You'll guide children as they explore what the Bible says about friendship, and get dozens of crowdbreaker and friend-maker activities.

Perfect for your Sunday school, Bible club, or after-school program!

ISBN 0-7644-2006-2

Order today from your local Christian bookstore, or write: Group Publishing, P.O. Box 485, Loveland, CO 80539